THE UNIVERSITY OF MICHIGAN TRIVIA

by Susan K. McCann

Quinlan Press
Boston

Copyright © 1986
by Quinlan Press
All rights reserved,
including the right of
reproduction in whole or
in part in any form.

Published by
Quinlan Press
131 Beverly Street
Boston, MA 02114

Library of Congress
Catalog Card Number 86-60715
ISBN 0-933341-48-2

Printed in the United States
of America, August 1986

For Dr. William John McCann, M.P.H. '69, and Dr. Joan Celia McCann, M.A. '68

Susan Kimberly McCann has many memories of Ann Arbor. She attended Ann Arbor public schools and later the University of Michigan, receiving a Master of Arts in Educational Technology in 1985. She is a 1984 Bachelor of Arts English graduate of the College of the Holy Cross in Worcester, Massachusetts, and is currently employed by the Children's Television Workshop. McCann resides in Pelham, New York.

Acknowledgments

To have the opportunity to research the history and traditions of the University of Michigan has filled me with awe as well as an overwhelming sense of incompleteness, for I realize that in one volume it is impossible to capture the many facts and legends that are stored in library archives or in the memories of Michigan alumni, professors and families.

The glorious spirit of Michigan can never be told in mere words. The story is more clearly echoed in the cheers of fans performing the "wave" at the Michigan Stadium, the ripples of the maize-and-blue flags along State Street, the whirr of the emergency helicopter landing at the University Hospital Medical Center, the glow of lights from the Law School Library, the conversations of students walking along the Diag, or the triumphant sound of the band playing "The Victors."

I acknowledge with sincere appreciation the time and interest in my project that was given to me by the dedicated staffs of the Bentley Historical Library, Ann Arbor Public Library, the University of Michigan Athletic Department Sports Information Office, the Alumni Association Center, University Tour Guides, Stats Services, the Center for Continuing Education of Women, and Quinlan Press.

I thank my family, friends and Michigan alumni who urged me on and gave me their

patient support, especially Pearl Graves, R.N., and my brother Peter, a 1986 Michigan State University graduate, who was able, at least temporarily, to forego all rivalries and leave behind East Lansing to assist me with my research in Ann Arbor.
 GO BLUE!

"Ann Arbor had happened to him, as it had happened to many. Ann Arbor had become home. And it still is."

> Milo Ryan, **View of a Universe: A Love Story of Ann Arbor at Middle Age,** 1985

CONTENTS

History, Legends and Traditions	1
Answers	16
The Victors	30
Answers	55
Sports, Spirit and Fans	60
Answers	88
The Wolverines	100
Answers	111
Campus Tour Guide	117
Answers	162
Mich Mosh	174
Answers	187

HISTORY, LEGENDS AND TRADITIONS

1. The University of Michigan has been known by two other names. What are they?

2. In what year was the school renamed the University of Michigan?

3. True or False: The birthplace of the University of Michigan was Ann Arbor.

4. Among state universities, the University of Michigan was established:
    a) third.
    b) tenth.
    c) fifteenth.
    d) first.

History, Legends and Traditions — Questions

5. In what year was the University of Michigan founded?
    a) 1808
    b) 1817
    c) 1837
    d) 1800

6. Who was the first graduate of the University to become its president?

7. What roles did Father Gabriel Richard and the Reverend John Monteith play in the history of the University of Michigan?

8. Who was the first president of the University of Michigan?

9. When did Ann Arbor become the home of the University of Michigan?

10. The University of Michigan received its first land grant from the _____ and the _____.

11. What do Collins, Goodrich, Norris, Parmelee, Pray and Wesson all have in common?

12. What special recognition did Wesson have?

13. Which two bestsellers of 1838 were the first to appear on the library shelves?

History, Legends and Traditions — Questions

14. In 1858, according to Dorothy Gies McGuigan, what did a Regents' report regard as a "Doubtful and Dangerous Experiment?"

15. Under whose administration was the resolution passed to accept women to the University of Michigan?

16. When was the first female student admitted to the University of Michigan?

17. Who was the first female student?

18. The first female student entered the University as a:
    a) medical student.
    b) freshman.
    c) music tutor.
    d) sophomore.

19. According to **A Dangerous Experiment**, which University of Michigan professor, soon to be president, favored a "Separate Facility," "Female Seminary," or "State College for Young Ladies" and called co-education a "Radical Revolution"?

20. In June 1859 a petition was signed by 1,476 citizens of Ann Arbor and presented to the Regents pleading

History, Legends and Traditions — Questions

that women:
  a) not be admitted to the school.
  b) live on a separate campus.
  c) be admitted to the University.
  d) be admitted only if they could live at home.

21. The first students were required to:
    a) iron their shirts.
    b) attend chapel from 5:30 a.m. to 6:30 a.m.
    c) chop wood for fire.
    d) secure meals from Ann Arbor residents.

22. Which Michigan president is known for holding an eleven-year administration, proposing classes for graduate students, and raising funds for an observatory?

23. True or False: President Henry Philip Tappan retired in Ann Arbor.

24. After whom was the Columbian organ, used at the Chicago Exposition of 1893, renamed?

25. Besides Latin teacher, what other position did Henry Simmons Frieze hold?

26. Which school was the first to admit women as students?

4

History, Legends and Traditions — Questions

    a) Harvard
    b) University of Michigan
    c) Yale
    d) College of the Holy Cross

27. Which graduate was a medical student in the early 1920s, the first dean of women, and the first female professor at the University?

28. Who was the first woman to receive a medical degree with honors from the University of Michigan (but was booed at her graduation ceremony)?

29. This 1893 medical graduate became a world-renowned authority on industrial medicine and the first woman on the faculty of Harvard. Who is she?

30. In order to become an assistant professor of industrial medicine at Harvard in 1919, what were the four conditions with which this University of Michigan graduate had to content herself?

31. What was the main demand of the faculty when they agreed to coeducation during the summer of 1870? In addition, what did the members of the Medical Department insist upon?

History, Legends and Traditions — Questions

32. Why was the University of Michigan called "the mother of state universities"?

33. What did a University of Michigan archaeological expedition in 1938 discover 2.5 miles off the shore of Heisterman Island?

34. True or False: The University of Michigan differed from other schools in that it was free from church control.

35. Which state university is closely linked to the founding of the University of Michigan?

36. What did the development of the above two systems of education have in common?

37. What do the Reverends George P. Williams and Joseph Whiting have in common?

38. What were the annual salaries of Father John Monteith and Father Gabriel Richard?

39. Who was Harriet Ada Patton?

40. What did the first female applicant, Sarah Burger of Ann Arbor, do when she was twice refused admission?

History, Legends and Traditions — Questions

41. This University of Michigan graduate entered the University in June 1872 at the age of 17. At 26, she became the youngest college president in the country, at Wellesley College. She received the first honorary doctor of philosophy degree ever presented to a woman. Who was this graduate?

42. What did 1875 graduate Olive San Louie Anderson, author of **An American Girl and Her Four Years in a Boys' College** (1878), burn as a sign of her female liberation?

43. With whom did Octavia Bates 1877, lawyer and activist in women's causes, have tea?

44. What occupation did graduate Annie Peck choose after she resigned from teaching?
    a) lawyer
    b) opera singer
    c) doctor
    d) mountain climber
What was her nickname?

45. The first women's club at the University of Michigan was called the Q.C.'s. Who was its founder?

7

History, Legends and Traditions — Questions

46. What do the club's letters stand for?
    a) Queen's Closet
    b) Quick Cooking
    c) Quiet Chatter
    d) None of the above

47. From 1871 to 1909 President Angell's administration promoted an increase in five areas of the University. Name these areas.

48. In what year did President Angell establish the summer school?

49. In 1921, 1882 law school graduate William W. Cook of New York gave sixteen million dollars to the University. Why?

50. What did Cook think of the result of his gift?

51. The School of Dentistry, established in 1875, was the _____ institution to offer education in dentistry in the world.
    a) twentieth
    b) second
    c) seventh
    d) thirteenth

52. What special recognition does the University of Michigan hold among dental schools?

8

History, Legends and Traditions — Questions

53. In what years were the first master of arts and doctor of philosophy degrees awarded?

54. What two criteria were essential to enter the law school?

55. To whom did the law class of 1864 dedicate a memorial statue in 1893?
    a) Abraham Lincoln
    b) Ben Franklin
    c) Ulysses S. Grant
    d) P.T. Barnum

56. Where is this statue located?
    a) Behind the President's House
    b) Next to the Harlan Hatcher Graduate Library
    c) In the Museum of Art
    d) None of the above

57. From what novel source did the University receive financial support?

58. In what year did the Department of Medicine and Surgery open? The Law Department?

59. In 1871, what special contribution did Professor Charles Kendall Adams, head of the history department, make to the University of Michigan and all universities of America?

History, Legends and Traditions — Questions

60. Which Michigan administration established the first permanent chair devoted to the professional training of teachers in the United States?

61. What was Woodrow Wilson's message of May 1918 to Dean M.E. Cooley of the College of Engineering?

62. What did Eikichi Araki, the Japanese ambassador to the United States, present to President Harlan Hatcher?

63. The _____ is regarded as one of the most perfectly equipped in the United States.

64. Professor Watson of the University of Michigan is best known for his discovery of _____.
   a) steam
   b) asteroids and comets
   c) surgical clamps
   d) Petoskey stones

65. Which of the following honors did Watson receive for his discoveries?
   a) A gold medal from the Imperial Academy of Sciences in Paris
   b) The patent and decoration of Knight Commander of the

History, Legends and Traditions — Questions

       Mejidich from the Khedive of Egypt in 1875
   c) Entrance into the Royal Academy of Sciences of Catania in Italy (1870)
   d) All of the above

66. Which University of Michigan history professor became the first president of Cornell University?

67. In 1860 a _____ was an unexpected visitor at the University chapel.
   a) python
   b) horse
   c) wolverine
   d) pig

68. Who is buried at the original University burying ground?

69. Which phrase appears on the University seal?
   a) Semper Fideles
   b) Pax Et Lux
   c) Artes, Scientia, Veritas
   d) Veritas

70. What did Noah Webster have in common with the University of Michigan?

71. On April 5, 1843, Major Jonathan Kearsley designed a University of Michigan seal, which was in use un-

History, Legends and Traditions — Questions

til 1895. Major Kearsley's design included a Latin motto:

"Minerva Monstrat Iter Quaque Ostendid Se Dextra Sequamur."

According to the 1951 **Michigan Alumnus**, all but the first word is from what source?

72. What do Horace Greeley, Mark Twain, P.T. Barnum, Eleanor Roosevelt, Ogden Nash, Bette Davis, Agnes DeMille, Lillian Gish, Marcel Marceau, Norman Vincent Peale and John Steinbeck have in common with the University of Michigan?

73. In 1922, what did H.E. Hastings and O.H. Clark build on both sides of South State Street?
    a) a bar
    b) a nine-hole golf course
    c) a baseball diamond
    d) a store

74. What do the titles **For the Love of Pete**, **Jane Climbs a Mountain**, **Thank You, Madam** and **Castles in Spain** have in common with the University of Michigan?

75. In 1860 when students stole the chapel bell, what was their punishment?
    a) Suspension
    b) Two-minute time limit to sign in for mandatory religious services

History, Legends and Traditions — Questions

    c) Expulsion
    d) No food for a day

76. What is unique about the chemical laboratory at the University of Michigan?

77. The following clause is important to the history of education and to the University of Michigan:
    > Religion, morality and knowledge being necessary to good government and the happiness of mankind, schools and the means of education shall forever be encouraged.

    In which document can this clause be found? On what University of Michigan building is this clause engraved?

78. What did former Michigan governor Chase S. Osborn present to the University after his trip around the world in 1913?

79. Translate the following original names of university departments:
    a) Anthropoglossica
    b) Mathematica
    c) Physiognostica
    d) Physiosophica
    e) Astronomia
    f) Chymia
    g) Iatuca
    h) Economia
    i) Ethica
    j) Polemitactica
    k) Diegetica
    l) Ennoeica

80. In 1841, what were the requirements for admission?

81. What was the tuition in the early days of the University of Michigan?

13

History, Legends and Traditions — Questions

82. The catalog of 1850 set the minimum age for admission at _____.

83. What were the requirements for admission to the medical school in 1850?

84. From the following description, what was a student attempting to develop in an early science class?
    > Our only resources were a junk bottle and a cigar box, and by hard work on a warm, dry day, we succeeded in obtaining a spark about as large as you can get in a dark room by stroking a black cat's back the wrong way.

85. Who was Sarah Killgore Wertman?

86. This 20th-century education reformist was head of the Department of Philosophy and lived at South University and Forest. Who is he?

87. Madelon Stockwell was the first woman to enter the University—as a sophomore. Who was the first freshman woman?

88. Through the efforts of Robert Frost, _____ magazine came into existence.

History, Legends and Traditions — Questions

89. The March 12, 1939, diary entry of Professor Harley Harris Bartlett states that a memorable walk in an ice storm through Ann Arbor led Frost to write what poem?

90. According to one interview, which three teaching devices did this poet employ while at the University?

91. What restrictions were placed on Robert Frost by the University administration?

92. What is the Mortar Board?

93. What was the result of an explosion in 1892 that blew out the windows of the first chemistry building?

94. For whom was Ann Arbor named?

ANSWERS

1. In 1817 the University of Michigan was known as the Catholespistemiad or the University of Michigania. Catholepistemia is defined "universal science."

2. 1821

3. False. The birthplace of the University of Michigan was Detroit, Michigan, on the corner of Larned and Bates Streets.

4. d) first—Michigan was the first state to establish a public university system.

5. b) The University of Michigan

History, Legends and Traditions — Answers

was founded in Detroit in 1817 (and incorporated in Ann Arbor in 1837).

6. Harry B. Hutchins, LL.D.

7. Father Gabriel Richard, pastor of St. Anne's Parish, and the Reverend John Monteith, an Episcopalian minister, helped charter the University of Michigan in 1817.

8. Reverend John Monteith, a young missionary and graduate of Princeton University, was the first president of the University of Michigan in Detroit. (Henry Philip Tappan was the first president in Ann Arbor.)

9. In 1837 the University moved to Ann Arbor and was redeveloped under the Board of Regents when Michigan joined the union.

10. Ann Arbor Land Company, Allen and Ann Rumsey farm

11. Judson D. Collins, Merchant H. Goodrich, Lyman D. Norris, George E. Parmelee, George W. Pray and William B. Wesson were the first students of the University of Michigan when classes began in the

History, Legends and Traditions — Answers

fall of 1841. They came from Lyndon Township, Ann Arbor (2), Ypsilanti, Superior and Detroit.

12. William B. Wesson was the only sophomore among the first students. All of the others entered as freshmen.

13. While in Europe, botanist and first Ann Arbor university faculty member Asa Gray was given five thousand dollars by the Regents to purchase books for the library. The first volume purchased was Audubon's **Birds of America**. The second volume, Brockhaus's **Konversations-Lexicon**, was a gift from a fur trader of the Upper Peninsula.

14. Co-education

15. Acting President Henry Simmons Frieze

16. February 1870

17. Madelon Stockwell. According to the **Michigan Alumnus**, comments about her include the following statement: "Her reading of the Latin text and translation were perfect, her answers to the questions on grammar prompt and cor-

History, Legends and Traditions — Answers

rect, a perfect recitation. It seemed to call for applause, and I only wish I had started it."

18. d) sophomore.

19. Professor Erastus Haven

20. c) be admitted to the university.

21. All but a

22. Henry Phillip Tappan, elected president in August 1852

23. False. Tappan's insistence on eliminating religious background as a qualification in the appointment of professors and on creating policies without faculty advice resulted in several arguments and criticisms. As a result, Tappan left for Europe in 1863 and never returned to Ann Arbor, or the United States.

24. The organ was renamed the Frieze Memorial Organ after Henry Simmons Frieze, a Latin professor, who organized the Choral Union and the University Musical Society.

25. Frieze was appointed acting president on August 1, 1871, during the administration of James Burrill Angell.

History, Legends and Traditions — Answers

26. b) University of Michigan

27. Dr. Eliza Mosher 1875

28. Dr. Amanda Sanford 1871 of Auburn, New York

29. Dr. Alice Hamilton 1893

30. 1) Low salary
    2) No Harvard Club privileges
    3) No football ticket privileges
    4) No commencement platform privileges

31. Five hundred dollars additional salary; separate instruction for male and female medical students

32. Because it was the largest and most successful; younger schools turned to it for guidance.

33. An Ottawa Village, untouched for over one hundred years, was discovered.

34. True. Only in its first years was the University influenced by religious ideas.

35. The University of Virginia. Judge Augustus A.B. Woodward, a scholar from Columbia University, was a friend of President Thomas

History, Legends and Traditions — Answers

Jefferson, who appointed him chief justice of the territory in 1805. Woodward visited Jefferson at Monticello in 1814 while he was developing the University of Virginia.

36. Both states proposed a complete system of education from elementary school to university, and both allowed for a central management board and allocated final control to the states.

37. The Reverend George P. Williams, an Episcopalian minister from Pontiac, and the Reverend Joseph Whiting, a Presbyterian minister from Niles, were the first two members of the faculty in Detroit.

38. President John Monteith received an annual salary of $25.00, and Father Richard received $18.75.

39. A graduate of Ann Arbor's Union High School who, in 1872, became the second woman to receive a law degree from the University

40. She began a career in the cause of women's rights.

41. Alice Freeman Palmer 1876

42. Her corset

History, Legends and Traditions — Answers

43. Queen Victoria of England

44. d) Mountain climber. Annie "Queen of the Climbers" Peck was one of three women in the 19th century to climb the Matterhorn. At 58, she scaled Mount Huascaron in Peru, which was named Cumbre Annie Peck. Supposedly, President Teddy Roosevelt read her book on mountain climbing.

45. Lucy Maynard Salmon 1876

46. d) None of the above. At present, there has been no record found of the meaning of Q.C.

47. Enrollment, faculty, library holdings, revenue sources and buildings. In these 38 years, the University grew from 1,207 to 5,223 students; 35 to 400 members of the faculty; 9 to 54 school buildings; 25,000 to 260,990 volumes in the library; and from a total increase of revenue of $104,000 to $11,170,000.

48. 1894

49. William W. Cook, general counsel for the Commercial Cable and Postal Telegraph Company, gave his gift to establish the Lawyers' Club, law dormitories and Martha

History, Legends and Traditions — Answers

Cook Dorm, and to aid the Michigan Law Review.

50. Unfortunately, Cook refused to see the law buildings until they were completed. He died of tuberculosis June 4, 1930, in Port Chester, New York, before their completion in 1933.

51. b) second

52. The dentistry building is the first building in the world devoted solely to graduate and postgraduate dental instruction.

53. 1849 and 1876, respectively

54. A student had to be eighteen years old and possess good moral character.

55. b) Ben Franklin

56. d) None of the above. The memorial statue of Ben Franklin stood on a stoop seventy-five feet from the southwest corner of the old law building. For several years, students pulling pranks painted Ben maize and blue. Found to be in the way of several baseball games, the statue mysteriously ended up in the boiler house.

History, Legends and Traditions — Answers

57. The University of Michigan received income from the tax of one-twentieth of a mill upon all taxable property in the state.

58. The Department of Medicine and Surgery opened in 1850, the Law Department in 1860.

59. He introduced the German Seminar method of education to the classroom.

60. The administration of James Burrill Angell

61. Woodrow Wilson noted the decrease in engineering students and stated that engineering duties were important in the Army and Navy, particularly for reconstruction after World War I.

62. On October 19, 1952, Eikichi Araki presented the University with 182 Japanese cherry trees during a three-week ceremony sponsored by the University's Japanese Festival.

63. The astronomical observatory. Constructed during President Tappan's administration and funded by the Honorable H.N. Walker of Detroit, the observatory was fur-

History, Legends and Traditions — Answers

nished with an achromatic refracting telescope, equatorial telescope and meridian circle, and was directed by the famous Dr. C. Brunnow of Berlin.

64. b) asteroids and comets

65. d) All of the above

66. Professor Andrew Dickson White, 1857-1867. He also served as the United States ambassador to Germany and Russia.

67. d) pig

68. No one. When Professor Whiting of the Language Department died, a monument was erected near the medical building but moved in 1884 because it interfered with baseball practice.

69. c) Artes, Scientia, Veritas

70. Noah Webster's 1829 "Blue Back Speller" received a frontspiece engraved by the earliest American engraver on wood, Alexander Anderson of New York. The design was identical with Michigan's old "Minerva Seal." In the Michigan version, Minerva is seated with a young student and is in modern costume.

History, Legends and Traditions — Answers

71. The second book of Virgil's **Aeneid**

72. They were all speakers for the University of Michigan Oratorical Association, which was created by Professor Emeritus Trueblood in 1888.

73. b) a nine-hole golf course

74. These were all plays written in the 1920s by female members of the junior class as a farewell to seniors.

75. b) Two-minute time-limit to sign in for mandatory religious services

76. It was the first laboratory established at a state university.

77. This clause is found in the Congress Provision Act of July 23, 1787, which is part of the Ordinance of 1787 for governing the Northwest Territory. The clause was the basis of the federal government and state university policy on education, and it is inscribed above the portico of Angell Hall.

78. The egg of an extinct, giant, flightless bird of Madagascar, the skeleton of an extinct pygmy hippopotamus, and a series of plaster casts of Bushmen drawings from the Cape Town Museum

History, Legends and Traditions — Answers

79. a) Literature
    b) Mathematics
    c) Natural history
    d) Natural philosophy
    e) Astronomy
    f) Chemistry
    g) Medical sciences
    h) Economical sciences
    i) Ethical sciences
    j) Military sciences
    k) Historical sciences
    l) Intellectual sciences

80. In August applicants for admission had to provide evidence of "good moral character, the elements of algebra, the grammar of the English, Latin, and Greek languages, and the readers of Andrews, Cornelius, Nepos, Vita Washingtonii, Sallust and Cicero's Oration."

81. The fees were "not to exceed $15.00 for a course of lectures."

82. fourteen

83. A knowledge of English grammar, rhetoric, literature, natural philosophy and mathematics, as well as a three-year internship with a physician

84. An electric battery

85. Sarah Killgore Wertman was the first woman graduate of the law

History, Legends and Traditions — Answers

school in 1871, the first woman to practice law in the United States and the first woman admitted to practice before the Supreme Court of Michigan.

86. John Dewey

87. Julia Knight Edwards

88. **Inlander**

89. "Brown's Descent"

90. The research laboratory, the studio apprenticeship and the "salon of goods minds"

91. None. He was "officially freed from all obligations to conform to any of the rules of that educational community.... No regular classes to meet, no routine duties, social or academic; nothing but the spur of his own spirit to prod him."

92. The Mortar Board is the national honor society of college seniors founded in 1918.

93. Professor E.D. Campbell went blind from the accident but appeared the next day with a bandage around his head and continued to

History, Legends and Traditions — Answers

teach for the next thirty-three years.

94. Ann Allen and Mary Ann Rumsey, the wives of the Ann Arbor founders

THE VICTORS

1. Which of the following original cast members of NBC's "Saturday Night Live" is a University of Michigan alumnus?
    a) Lorraine Newman
    b) Chevy Chase
    c) Gilda Radner
    d) Jane Curtin

2. Alumnus _____ graduated in 1970 and received a Master of Arts degree in 1972. He was the screenwriter and/or director for **The Big Chill**, **Body Heat**, **Raiders of the Lost Ark** and **Return of the Jedi**.

3. Kurt Luedtke '51 was the screen-

The Victors — Questions

writer for which of the following films?
   a) **The Right Stuff**
   b) **Trip to Bountiful**
   c) **Chapter Two** and **The Goodbye Girl**
   d) **Absence of Malice** and **Out of Africa**

4. This member of the Class of 1948 received a Master of Arts degree in 1949 and was the TV producer of "Maude," "That Girl" and "Mayberry RFD." Who is he?

5. This alumnus composed the song "Happy Days Are Here Again." Who is he?

6. _____ received a Master of Business Administration in 1957 and is the former president of the DeLorean Motor Company.

7. Match the alumnus with the university of which he or she is president:

1) Matina Souretis Horner, M.S. '63, Ph.D. '68
2) Edward Jennings, Ph.D. '69
3) John A. DiBiaggio, M.A. '67

a) Michigan State University
b) Ohio State University
c) Radcliffe College

8. This singer/actress attended the University of Michigan from 1978 to 1979 and is noted for the album "Like a Virgin," the movie "Desperately Seeking Susan," and her

The Victors — Questions

marriage to Sean Penn. She lived in East Quad. Who is she?

9. This 1939 graduate was an announcer for the University radio station and a member of the Phi Epsilon Pi fraternity. In 1956 he anchored "Night Beat," an hour-long news and interview show, and hosted an intern program for ABC in 1957. He wrote a column for the **New York Post**, co-hosted the 1961 Westinghouse production of "P.M. East," and anchored the "CBS Morning News" in 1963. Today, he co-hosts "60 Minutes" and is the author of **Close Encounters**. Who is he?

10. In 1874 this alumnus studied qualitative analysis at the chemical laboratory of the University of Michigan. He was editor of the "Good Health" journal for more than seventy years, founder of the Battle Creek Sanitorium, and the inventor of packaged corn flakes, granola and peanut butter. Who is he?

11. He received a Masters in Business Administration in 1969 and starred in the television series "Barney Miller." Which character did he portray?

The Victors — Questions

12. This 1980 graduate is a Broadway actor and dancer who was seen in "On Your Toes" and "Singing in the Rain," in the Donald O'Connor role. Who is he?

13. Which of the following television programs did alumnus Henry Coleman produce?
    a) "Hotel"
    b) "Love Boat"
    c) "Peyton Place"
    d) "Dr. Kildare"
    e) "That Girl"

14. Roger L. Stevens attended the University of Michigan from 1928 until 1930 and held which of the following positions?
    a) Producer of **West Side Story** and **Cat on a Hot Tin Roof**
    b) Chairperson of The Kennedy Center in Washington, D.C.
    c) Producer of **A Man for All Seasons**
    d) Producer of **Annie**
    e) All of the above

15. This novelist and poet of the Class of 1957 wrote **Braided Lives** and **Fly Away Home**. Who is she?

16. Leonard Michaels, A.M. '57, Ph.D. '67, is best known for what novel?

The Victors — Questions

17. Nicki McWhirter of the Class of 1951 is a journalist and columnist for which of the following newspapers?
    a) **Ann Arbor News**
    b) **Boston Globe**
    c) **Detroit Free Press**
    d) **New York Times**

18. This 1952 graduate served as brigadier general for the United States Marine Corps. Who is she?

19. _____ of the Class of 1940 was the former vice president of the Associated Press.

20. This 1916 law graduate was the former Secretary of the Army in the 1950s. Who is he?

21. _____ graduated in 1970, received a Master of Arts degree in 1971, and works as a foreign correspondent for the **London Times**.

22. This 1975 graduate is a journalist and writes celebrity profiles for several magazines. Who is he?

23. William Shawn attended the University of Michigan from 1925 until 1927 and was an editor for which of the following magazines?
    a) **New Yorker**

b) **Better Homes and Gardens**
c) **People**
d) **Time**

24. _____ of the Class of 1959 served as the White House deputy press secretary in the Eisenhower administration.

25. This graduate received a Ph.D. in 1966 and a J.D. in 1970. She served as deputy secretary of the Department of Health, Education and Welfare and also on the Commission on Civil Rights. Who is she?

26. This member of the Class of 1953 received an LL. B. in 1956. He is a journalist for the **Washington Post** and a Pulitzer Prize recipient. Who is he?

27. What do Thomas H. Weller '36, M.S. '37; Samuel C. Ting '59, M.S. '60, Ph.D. '63; and Marshall W. Nirenberg, Ph.D. '57, have in common?

28. Carl Gerstacker received an engineering degree in 1938. Of which corporation was he chairman?

29. Which 1930 graduate is associated

35

The Victors — Questions

with the Dow Jones and the **Wall Street Journal**?

30. This 1883 medical graduate founded the Mayo Clinic in Minnesota. Who is he?

31. _____ of the Class of 1931 served as chairman of the General Motors Corporation.

32. This 1922 graduate was a governor of New York and a 1948 presidential candidate. Who is he?

33. Ray T. Parfet, Jr., M.B.A. '47, was chairman and chief executive officer of which of the following companies?
   a) The Upjohn Company
   b) IBM
   c) General Electric
   d) Marine Midland Bank

34. This 1878 law graduate, 1902 member of the Illinois legislature, and author of **An Eye for An Eye** and **Resist Not Evil** was involved in the Scopes Monkey Trial and the Leopold-Loeb trial. Who is he?

35. For which residence on Pennsylvania Avenue was 1956 medical graduate William M. Lukasit the chief physician in 1974?

The Victors — Questions

36. _____, who received his Masters in Business Administration in 1950, is chairman of Comerica, Inc.

37. Match the following list of alumni with their careers:

1) Roger B. Smith '48, M.B.A. '53
2) Stanley Winkelman '43
3) E. Grifford Upjohn '26, M.D. '28
4) Harold K. Sperlich '51, M.B.A. '61
5) Lawrason D. Thomas, M.B.A. '58
6) Charles Walgreen, Ph.C '28, Hon. M.S. '51
7) Ruth Hussey, 1933-1934
8) Robert Q. Lewis '41
9) Mary Joan Negro '70
10) Milan Stitt '63
11) Jonathan Shames '82
12) Jessye Norman '68
13) Margaret Bourke White, 1922-1924
14) William Milliken, Hon. Law '67
15) William Briggs Macharg, 1892-1895
16) William Randolph Mills, 1914-1915
17) Henry Thomas Thurber, 1874
18) Nathan White '79

a) Stage and film actress
b) Playwright of **The Runner Stumbles**, faculty member UM
c) Actor and comedian for stage and television
d) Chairperson and chief executive officer of the General Motors Corporation
e) President of the Chrysler Corporation
f) World's leading soprano
g) Film director and screenwriter for **The Carrier**
h) President of Amoco
i) Stage and television actress
j) Photographer and journalist
k) Concert pianist and conductor
l) Chairperson of Winkelman Stores
m) Founder of Walgreen Drugstores
n) Chairperson of the Upjohn Corporation
o) Author of **The Indian Drum**, 1917
p) Former governor of Michigan, 1969-1980, and Zeta Psi fraternity member
q) Private secretary to Grover Cleveland, 1893
r) NBC musical director; "Fibber Magee and Molly" radio announcer

37

The Victors — Questions

38. This 1867 law graduate was the United States postmaster general from 1888 to 1898 and chief advisor to Grover Cleveland. Who is he?

39. Name the source of this statement:
    I played football on three great Michigan Varsity teams. Two were Big Ten and National Championship Squads and the third won only one game. But all three were great because all of them were played in the tradition of Michigan. It was an inspiration to me and I have found this same ingredient—inspiration, a large amount of enthusiasm—is an indispensable element of success in politics as well as football. My years at Michigan enriched my life.

40. Which of the following qualities are true about this graduate?
    a) He was a member of Delta Kappa Epsilon fraternity.
    b) He played center on the 1932, 1933 and 1934 football teams.
    c) He played for the Wolverines when they were national champs in 1932 and 1933.
    d) He captained the Varsity in 1934.

e) He was elected by his teammates as Most Valuable Player in 1934.
f) He was presented the Michigan Hall of Honor Award by the University of Michigan Department of Intercollegiate Athletics on August 9, 1978, in recognition of outstanding service to the University in "athletics and life."
g) He received the Theodore Roosevelt Award, the highest honor conferred by the National Collegiate Athletic Association in 1975.
h) He served as the 38th President of the United States from 1974 to 1977.
i) All of the above

41. What do Robert Griffin, J.D. '50; Philip A. Hart, J.D. '37; Nancy Kassebaum, M.A. '56; and Donald Reigle '60 have in common?

42. What distinction does Nancy Kassebaum hold?

43. This 1896 law graduate served as the United States Secretary of the Navy from 1921 to 1924. Who is he?

The Victors — Questions

44. _____ of the Class of 1937 served as composer and music director of **Dream Wife** and **Gigi**.

45. This 1936 law graduate was governor of Michigan and a state supreme court judge. Who is he?

46. Mitzi M. Wertheim '60 served as deputy undersecretary of the ____.

47. A student at the University of Michigan from 1882 to 1883, this graduate worked as a United States Supreme Court justice from 1922 to 1938. Who is he?

48. Match the actor or actress on the left with his or her credits on the right:

   1) James Earl Jones '53
   2) Ken Marshall '72, M.A. '73
   3) Marian Mercer '57
   4) Martha Scott '32
   5) Reid Shelton '50

   a) **Annie**
   b) "Mary Hartman, Mary Hartman" and "Nine to Five," and a Tony Award winner for Best Supporting Actress in **Promises, Promises**
   c) **The Great White Hope** and **Othello**
   d) **Marco Polo**
   e) **Ben Hur**

49. What do Roberta Alexander '71 and Russell Christopher '54 have in common?

50. Ara Berberian '52, LL.B. '55; Ashley Putnam '74, Master in Music

The Victors — Questions

'75; and Noell Rogers '66 share the same profession. What is it?

51. This 1969 music school graduate is a composer and film scorer. Who is she?

52. Barbara Nissman received a Master of Arts in 1966 and a D.M.A. in 1969. What is her profession?

53. This 1870 graduate served as secretary of state in 1898 and as a United States Supreme Court justice from 1902 to 1923. Who is he?

54. Law school graduate _____ '12 served as the United States secretary of the treasury from 1953 to 1957.

55. What do Martha B. Segar '54, M.B.A. '55, and Nancy Hays Tecter, M.A. '54, have in common?

56. Martha Griffiths, J.D. '40, was a lieutenant governor for the state of _____.

57. _____, J.D. '62, is a member of the United States Court of Appeals, 2nd Circuit.

58. Cornelia Kennedy '45, J.D. '47, is a United States _____.

The Victors — Questions

59. Frank Murphy, LL.B. '14, LL.D. '39, was a _____.

60. This 1961 graduate is a California state representative, a former member of the Chicago 7, a founder of Students for a Democratic Society, a former editor of the **Michigan Daily**, and the husband of Jane Fonda. What is his name?

61. This 1951 graduate received a Master of Arts degree in 1952 and is a screenwriter and novelist. He received an Academy Award for the film **Gandhi**. Who is he?

62. Herbert Brodkin '33, M.A. '34, was the producer for which of the following TV shows?
    a) "The Defenders"
    b) "Playhouse 90"
    c) "Sakharov"
    d) "Skokie"
    e) "Holocaust"
    f) All of the above

63. Lisa Gottlieb, B.S.G. '84, was the film director of _____.

64. _____ '54 is the producer of the NBC Nightly News.

65. Josh Greenfeld '49 was the screenwriter of _____.

The Victors — Questions

66. Hal Cooper of the Class of 1946 was the producer and/or director for which of the following television programs?
    a) "Leave It to Beaver"
    b) "The Dick Van Dyke Show"
    c) "Mayberry R.F.D."
    d) "All in the Family"
    e) "That Girl"
    f) All of the above

67. This 1965 graduate wrote **Modigliani** and **Split Second**. Who is he?

68. Max Hodge '39, wrote for which of the following television programs:
    a) "The Wild, Wild West"
    b) "Battlestar Gallactica"
    c) "Marcus Welby"
    d) "The Waltons"
    e) "Kojak"
    f) All of the above

69. Alumni David and Leslie _____ '59 were the screenwriters for **Superman I**, **II** and **III**, **Bonnie and Clyde**, **What's Up, Doc?**, **Still of the Night** and **Santa Claus**.

70. The screenwriter of **For Whom the Bell Tolls**, this member of the Class

43

The Victors — Questions

of 1917 won the 1935 Best Screenplay Academy Award for **The Informer**. Name him.

71. Richard Lees '70 was the playwright and screenwriter of _____.

72. Screenwriter and playwright Paul Osborn '23, M.A. '24, wrote the scripts for which of the following films and plays?
    a) **East of Eden**
    b) **Sayonara**
    c) **The Yearling**
    d) **Mrs. Miniver**
    e) **South Pacific**
    f) **Morning's at Seven**
    g) All of the above

73. This 1963 graduate and poet received a Ph.D. in 1970 and wrote **Zip**, **Free Agents** and **The Oranging of America**. Who is he?

74. _____ of the Class of 1940 wrote **Somebody Up There Likes Me**, **The Night They Raided Minsky's** and **Harpo Speaks**.

75. Malcolm Bosse, M.A. '56, wrote the novels _____ and _____.

76. This 1969 graduate is a journalist and novelist who wrote **The Chosen Prey**. Who is he?

The Victors — Questions

77. Poet _____, M.A. '39, was a critic and poetry editor of the "Saturday Review." He wrote **A Browser's Dictionary**, **Selected Poems** (1984), **The Birds of Pompeii** (1985), **Doodle Soup** (1985) and an English translation of Dante's **Inferno**.

78. _____, poetry editor of the **New Yorker**, attended Michigan from 1939 to 1940.

79. _____ of the Class of 1971 is a journalist and White House media liaison officer.

80. Betsy Canter '67 is an editor for which of the following magazines?
    a) **Time**
    b) **Esquire**
    c) **House Beautiful**
    d) **Ms.**

81. Which 1925 graduate was the founder and publisher of **Esquire**?

82. _____ of the Class of 1955 wrote **Dr. Love** and is a restaurant critic for **New York** Magazine.

83. This 1950 graduate wrote **In the Freud Archives**. Who is she?

45

The Victors — Questions

84. This famous novelist, M.A. '42, Ph.D. '52, wrote the Lew Archer series. Who is he?

85. George Lichty '29 was the cartoonist for "Grin and Bear It." What was his real name?

86. Morton Frank '33 was the president and publisher of which of the following publications?
    a) **Vogue**
    b) **Smithsonian**
    c) **Family Weekly**
    d) **Reader's Digest**

87. **Life With Father** was written by journalist and novelist _____ of the Class of 1933.

88. Jennifer Levin '77 is the journalist and novelist who wrote _____ and _____.

89. This novelist and poet wrote **Ordinary People** and **Second Heaven**. Who is she?

90. Who is Cathy Guisewite, Class of 1972 and Tri Delt?

91. Leon Jaroff '50 is the editor of which publication?
    a) **Discover** Magazine
    b) **Life**

46

The Victors — Questions

    c) **Chicago Herald-Tribune**
    d) **Hartford Courant**

92. Carmen Harlan '75 is a television journalist and news anchor for _____.

93. What profession do John Malcolm Brinnin '42 and Robert Hayden share?

94. _____ '40 is a novelist and short-story writer who wrote **Out Went the Candle** and **Nights in the Gardens of Brooklyn**.

95. Law graduate Robert Traver '28 wrote **Anatomy of a Murder**. What was his real name?

96. Chris Von Allsburg '72 is an illustrator and writer of children's literature. She wrote **The Wreck of the Zypher** and **Jumanji**, for which she won a _____.

97. What member of the Class of 1962 wrote **A Boy's Own Story**?

98. Who developed the polio vaccine?

99. Name the source of this passage:
We'd come to think of them in terms of the professions they were studying for. Doctors, lawyers, engineers,

The Victors — Questions

lits. Lits! Long before I knew what a lit was I'd decided for myself it was a worthless thing to become. Trying to find a job as a lit was just a bit short of nonsense. Who would hire an author? Years afterward, when I myself entered, pursued, and was graduated from Lit, I thought many times of that childhood opinion, marveled at its precocious wisdom, and wished I'd been guided by it—especially as I watched some of my contemporaries become practicing lawyers, doctors or engineers and seemingly prosper young.

100. What profession of Karl Henize, Ph.D. '55, James A McDivitt '59, James B. Irwin, M.S. '57, Jack R. Lousma '59, David R. Scott, 1917-1918, Edward H. White, M.S.E. '59, and Alfred M. Worden, M.S.E. '63, have in common?

101. Who challenged Carl Levin for a seat in the Senate and flew on Skylab?

102. _____ was the first United States citizen to walk in space.

103. This alumnus served as commander on the first space shuttle and three others. Who is he?

The Victors — Questions

104. _____ was the commander of Gemini IV.

105. Constance Rosenblum wrote in her 1985 **New York Times** article: "Funny things happen to _____ when she gets into a movie. She starts off as a second banana—or at most co-banana. Then, the moment the film opens, critics and audience agree very quickly that she has all but stolen the show."

106. This actress (above) began her television career with the words, "I can see myself." In which commercial did she make her debut?

107. _____ '58, Ph.D. '63, is a poet and writer of children's literature. She wrote **A Visit to William Blake's Inn**, winner of the Newbery Award. She authored **Things Invisible to See** (1941), the love story of Ben Harkissian, star pitcher for Ann Arbor High School, and Clare Bishop, a young girl who is paralyzed by his baseball.

108. What award is presented yearly at the university to authors who produce plays, poetry, novels and essays that are "new, unusual and radical"?

The Victors — Questions

109. Name the source of this passage:
Nobody dast blame this man. You don't understand: Willy was a salesman. And for a salesman, there is no rock bottom to the life. He don't put a bolt to a nut, he don't tell you the law or give you medicine. He's a man way out there in the blue, riding on a smile and a shoeshine. And when they start not smiling back—that's an earthquake. And then you get yourself a couple of spots on your hat, and you're finished. Nobody dast blame this man. A salesman is got to dream, boy. It comes with the territory.

110. Name the source of this passage:
The one tree in Francie's yard was neither a pine nor a hemlock. It had pointed leaves which grew along green switches which radiated from the bough and made a tree which looked like a lot of opened green umbrellas. Some people called it the Tree of Heaven. No matter where its seed fell, it made a tree which struggled to reach the sky. It grew in boared-up lots and out of neglected rubbish heaps and it was the only tree that grew out of cement. It grew lushly, but only in the tenement districts.

111. What unusual circumstances regarded the enrollment of this alumna (above)?

The Victors — Questions

112. This 1935 alumnus saved an estimated 100,000 Hungarian Jews from Nazi death camps in Budapest during World War II but never returned from Soviet imprisonment. NBC aired a two-part miniseries, starring Richard Chamberlain, on his life. Who is he?

113. Which 1922-1924 University student studied herpetology under Professor Alexander G. Ruthven; took pictures for the **Michiganensian**; belonged to Alpha Omicron Pi sorority; kept a pet snake in her room; and is best known for the cover photograph and lead story of the first issue of **Life** Magazine, November 23, 1936?

114. This 1955 business graduate received an M.B.A. in 1956 and serves as vice president and executive producer of The Children's Television Workshop programs "Sesame Street" and "The Electric Company." Who is he?

115. For what accomplishment did Dr. Jerome Karle, M.S. '42, Ph.D. '43, win the 1985 Nobel Prize in chemistry?

116. Which 1974 graduate was the third woman in the United States to write for **Time's** "Nation" section?

The Victors — Questions

117. Which 1954 Ph.D. graduate was the oldest astronaut ever to fly in space? How old was he?

118. This 1928 graduate received a D.D.S. from the School of Dentistry in 1931, an M.S. in oral surgery in 1932 and an M.D. from the Medical School in 1936, and was internationally reknowned as a pioneer of modern maxillofacial reconstructive surgery. Who is he?

119. Which 1933 Ph.D. graduate and University of Michigan professor emeritus of botany wrote **The Mushroom Hunter's Field Guide** in 1958?

120. Name five plays written by University graduate Arthur Miller.

121. Which 1950 graduate and Avery Hopwood Award winner was a speechwriter for President Gerald R. Ford, Lee Iaccoca, Michigan senator Robert Griffin, and Michigan governors George Romney and William Milliken?

122. Which University graduate won a Pulitzer Prize and composed **Songs, Drones and Refrains of Death** and **Star-Child: A Parable for Soprano, Antiphonal Chil-**

dren's Voices and Large Orchestra?

123. She served as chairperson of President Nixon's Task Force on Women's Rights and Responsibilities in 1969 and as deputy assistant to the Secretary of State for Public Affairs (1972-1977). Who is this recipient of the Outstanding Achievement Award at the University of Michigan in 1964?

124. He served as medical professor of physiology and chairman of the bioengineering program at the University. He was the recipient of the Outstanding Research Award from the Michigan Heart Association in 1960 and was editor-in-chief of the International Journal of Biomedical Engineering. Name him.

125. _____ received a Masters in Music in 1960 and served as chorus master and conductor for the New York City Opera (1964-1969), conductor of the National Ballet in Washington (1970), conductor of the Eastman Philharmonic School of Music (1977), and music director of the Merola Program of the San Francisco Opera (1978-1979).

The Victors — Questions

126. This University graduate was the executive producer for the National Geographic Television special series "The Planet Earth," for which he won an Emmy in 1979 and a Peabody Award in 1980. Who is he?

127. This graduate offered the first formal full-semester course in forestry in the United States in the School of Political Science at the University from 1882 to 1885. Who is he?

ANSWERS

1. c) Gilda Radner

2. Lawrence Kasdan

3. d) **Absence of Malice** and **Out of Africa**

4. John Rich

5. Jack S. Yellen

6. John Z. DeLorean

7. 1) c
   2) b
   3) a

8. Madonna

The Victors — Answers

9. Mike Wallace

10. Dr. John Harvey Kellogg

11. Alumnus Maxwell Gail played Sergeant Wojohowitz.

12. Peter Slutsker

13. a, b, c and d

14. e) All of the above

15. Marge Piercy

16. **The Men's Club**

17. c) **Detroit Free Press**

18. Margaret A. Brewer

19. Stanley M. Swinton

20. William M. Brucker

21. Robin Wright

22. Tony Schwartz

23. a) **New Yorker**

24. Karna Small

25. Mary Francis Berry

26. Roger Wilkins

The Victors — Answers

27. They each are the recipient of a Nobel Prize.

28. Dow Corporation

29. William F. Kerby

30. William J. Mayo

31. Richard Gerstenberg

32. Thomas Dewey

33. The Upjohn Company

34. Clarence Darrow

35. The White House

36. Donald R. Mandich

37. 1) d   10) b
    2) l   11) k
    3) n   12) s
    4) e   13) j
    5) h   14) p
    6) m   15) o
    7) a   16) r
    8) c   17) q
    9) i   18) k

38. Don M. Dickinson

39. Gerald R. Ford '35

40. i) All of the above

The Victors — Answers

41. They were all United States senators.

42. Nancy Kassebaum was the only senator representing Kansas; the rest represented Michigan.

43. Edwin Denby

44. Charles Wolcott

45. G. Mennen Williams

46. Navy

47. George Sutherland

48. 1) c
    2) d
    3) b
    4) e
    5) a

49. They are both singers with the Metropolitan Opera in New York.

50. They are all opera singers.

51. Carol K. Lees

52. Concert pianist

53. William R. Day

54. George M. Humphrey

The Victors — Answers

55. They were both governors of the Federal Reserve Board.

56. Michigan

57. Amalya Kearse

58. judge

59. U.S. Supreme Court justice

60. Thomas Hayden

61. John Briley

62. f) All of the above

63. **Just One of the Guys**

64. Paul Greenberg

65. **Harry and Tonto**

66. b, c and e

67. Dennis McIntyre

68. a, c and d

69. Newman

70. Dudley Nichols

71. **Right of Way**

72. g) All of the above

59

The Victors — Answers

73. Max Apple
74. Rowland Barber
75. **The Warlord, Fire in Heaven**
76. William Brashler
77. John Ciardi
78. Howard Moss
79. Susan Mathis
80. b) **Esquire**
81. Arnold Gingrich
82. Gael Greene
83. Janet Malcolm
84. Ross MacDonald
85. Maurice Lichtenstein
86. c) **Family Weekly**
87. Frank B. Gilbreath
88. **Water Dancer** and **Snow**
89. Judith Guest '58
90. The cartoonist who developed

The Victors — Answers

"Cathy." Her books include **Another Saturday Night of Wild and Reckless Abandon** and **It Must Be Love, My Face is Breaking Out**

91. a) **Discover** Magazine

92. WDIV-Detroit

93. They are both poets.

94. Harvey Swados

95. John Voelker

96. Caldecott Medal

97. Edmund White

98. Jonas Salk

99. Milo Ryan in **View of a Universe: A Love Story of Ann Arbor at Middle Age**

100. They are all astronauts.

101. Jack Lousma

102. Edward White

103. Robert Crippen

104. James McDiVitt

The Victors — Answers

105. Christine Lahti

106. Joy Dishwashing Liquid

107. Nancy Willard

108. The James Avery Hopwood Award

109. Charley to Biff in **Death of a Salesman:** "The Requiem," by Arthur Miller '38

110. **A Tree Grows in Brooklyn**, by Betty Smith, winner of the James Avery Hopwood Award for playwriting

111. Betty Smith lacked a high school diploma when she applied for admission to the university. Dr. Clarence Cook Little and Professor Peter M. Jack arranged for her to enter as a special student. She received her degree after completing ten years of undergraduate work.

112. Raoul Wallenberg

113. Margaret Bourke-White

114. David D. Connell

115. He performed research that led to the universally accepted method of

deducing the molecular structure of crystals.

116. Ellie McGrath

117. Karl Henize; fifty-eight

118. Reed O. Dingman, Professor Emeritus of Surgery at the Medical School

119. Alexander H. Smith

120. **Incident at Vichy**
 After the Fall
 The Misfits
 All My Sons
 Death of a Salesman
 The Crucible
 A Memory of Two Mondays
 A View From the Bridge

121. George Lee Walker, author of **The Chronicles of Doodah**

122. George Crumb, D.M.A. '60

123. Virginia Rachel Allan, A.B. '39, M.A. Fellow '45

124. Peter Herman Abbrecht, M.S. '53, Ph.D. Chemical Engineering '57, M.D. '62

125. David Louis Effron

The Victors — Answers

126. Thomas Skinner, M.A. '57, Ph.D. '62

127. Volney Morgan Spalding, A.B. 1873

SPORTS, SPIRIT AND FANS

1. During the 1985 football season, how many hot dogs were consumed by Wolverine fans?

2. How many boxes of popcorn were consumed?

3. A Michigan club received top billing in a 1950 film. Which club was bestowed this honor?
   a) The Honors Society
   b) The Dramatic Club
   c) The Faculty Association
   d) The Glee Club

4. The first public appearance of the University of Michigan band took place at the _____.

Sports, Spirit and Fans — Questions

5. As a practice hall, the first band used _____.
   a) The Ann Arbor High School
   b) Harris Hall, over Calkin's Drug Store
   c) The hall of the Washtenaw Times Band, over Hutzel and Company Plumbing Shop on South Main Street
   d) All of the above

6. From 1927 to 1984, how many fans have watched the Wolverine football team play?

7. How many football games have fans watched during this time period?

8. What is the greatest number of people to watch a Wolverine game, and who were the Wolverines playing?

9. How many people attended games during the 1979 football season?

10. In 1984, what was the largest record of people to attend an away game?
    a) 80,024
    b) 84,685
    c) 100,093
    d) 90,286

Sports, Spirit and Fans — Questions

11. Where was this stadium record made?
    a) Ohio State
    b) Iowa
    c) Michigan State
    d) Minnesota

12. How many Rose Bowl games has the University of Michigan attended?
    a) Eleven
    b) Fifteen
    c) Eight
    d) Twenty

13. The University of Michigan played in the very first Rose Bowl game at Tournament Park in Pasadena, California. The University of Michigan won, 49-0. Who was the loser?

14. The Wolverines have played in Rose Bowl games with all but one of the following teams. Which team is it?
    a) USC
    b) Minnesota
    c) Oregon State
    d) California
    e) Washington

15. In 1976 80,037 fans watched Michigan play against Oklahoma in what bowl game?

Sports, Spirit and Fans — Questions

16. Michigan played in the Gator Bowl in 1979 with 70,407 fans in attendance. Who was its opponent?

17. In 1984 in front of 61,243 fans, Michigan played Brigham Young in the _____ Bowl.

18. In what year did Michigan play UCLA in the Blue Bonnet Bowl, with 50,107 fans watching?

19. Michigan played in the Sugar Bowl against _____ in 1984, with 77,893 fans watching.

20. What team did Michigan play in the Fiesta Bowl at the Sun Devil Stadium on January 1, 1986?

21. Who was the quarterback for Michigan during that game?

22. Name the source of the following statement:
    > If we win it, the players all realize it's in spite of the coaches. Whatever it takes to win bowl games, I ain't got it. It's kind of an albatross around my neck, but it isn't going to make or break my career. I've already established I can't win bowl games.

Sports, Spirit and Fans — Questions

23. After winning the Fiesta Bowl, what is this coach's bowl game record?

24. On January 1, 1986, an NBC sportscaster stated, "It is tradition that one must get through the Wolverines and _____ to win the Big Ten."

25. Match the team on the left with the years on the right in which it played Michigan in the Rose Bowl:

　1) USC　　　　　　　a) 1902, 1972
　2) Washington　　　b) 1951
　3) Stanford　　　　　c) 1965
　4) Oregon State　　d) 1978, 1981
　5) California　　　　e) 1948, 1970, 1977, 1979, 1983

26. Since 1975, the University of Michigan football team has had a crowd of at least _____ people at each home game and has led the United States in attendance.

27. What was the first football game at which the University of Michigan band played?

28. Which University of Michigan football player was called "Old 98" and wore breakaway jerseys to escape tacklers?

29. How many jerseys did he use in his football career?

Sports, Spirit and Fans — Questions

30. He is the father of "St. Elsewhere" star _____.

31. What did Francis, Albert, and Alvin have in common?
    a) The last name Wistert
    b) The number eleven
    c) All-American football titles
    d) all of the above

32. Why were the Michigan football teams of 1901 to 1905 called the "Point-a-Minute" teams?

33. Which University of Michigan football star played himself in the movie **Crazylegs**?

34. In 1982, how many winning team titles did Michigan have? How many individual titles?

35. Which University of Michigan athlete twice won the Broderick Award, given by the Association for Intercollegiate Athletics for Women to outstanding collegiate women athletes of the year in championship sports?

36. True or False: The following activities are officially accepted by the 1986 Department of Recreational Sports:
    a) Soaring

Sports, Spirit and Fans — Questions

    b) Square dancing
    c) Water polo
    d) Cricket
    e) Kayaking

37. Dick Hanley placed second in the 800m relay and fifth in the 100m freestyle for the _____ Olympic team.

38. In 1936 Taylor Drysdale placed fourth for the US Olympic Team in what event?

39. Dick Deneger won a gold medal in the 1932 Olympics—for which event?

40. Who placed second in springboard diving on the 1948 Olympic Team and served as high diving coach at the University from 1955 to 1959?

41. Robert Sohl placed third in what event during the 1948 Olympics?

42. Who coined the term "Field House"?

43. What is the tradition of the "Little Brown Jug," and to whom did the Minneapolis Rotary Club give permanent possession of the jug, November 8, 1940?

Sports, Spirit and Fans — Questions

44. Who was football's "first linebacker"? What honor was he bestowed in 1951 and 1969?

45. Which UM halfback never played in a losing game and is considered to be one of the greatest scorers in college history?

46. Which baseball player played for both the Los Angeles Dodgers and the St. Louis Cardinals and was the 1969 National League Rookie of the Year?

47. Who was Henry "Hank" Hatch, and what was his connection to the tradition of the Little Brown Jug?

48. This University of Michigan athlete won nine letters in football, baseball and basketball and is the only three-time football All-American. He was an All-American leading Big Ten scorer and conference hitter in baseball and was the top amateur athlete in 1927. He also coached Michigan basketball for nine years and football for eleven seasons and was awarded the Coach of the Year Award in 1948. Who is he?

49. This person served as head football coach from 1938 to 1948 and was

athletic director from 1941 to 1968. He twice enlarged the Michigan stadium, constructed the Matt Mann Pool, built the Women's Indoor Swimming Pool, renovated the baseball stadium, and constructed the Michigan Golf Course. He won two Big Ten titles, the national championship in 1947, and led his team to victory in the 1948 Rose Bowl over USC, 49-0. He authored **Practical Football** (1933) and **Modern Football** (1949). Who is he?

50. Which University of Michigan coach served the school for forty-five years, coached wrestling and football, and obtained a law degree in 1933?

51. In what years was the gymnastics team NCAA gymnastics champs?
    a) 1950 and 1961
    b) 1930 and 1945
    c) 1963 and 1970
    d) 1955 and 1962

52. Which basketball player succeeded in completing the following feats?
    — A 20-foot jumpshot resulting in a score of Michigan 60, Indiana 59, February 10, 1979
    — A 19-foot jumpshot leaving the score Michigan 68, Min-

Sports, Spirit and Fans — Questions

nesota 67, January 10, 1981
- A last-minute layup shot allowing Michigan to win over Michigan State 79-77, February 5, 1981
- Three game-winning free throws in overtime resulting in a Michigan 55, Indiana 52 score January 15, 1981

53. What did the Class of 1870 set up in 1868 that Kent Sagendorph referred to as a "gymnasium in embryo?"

54. What was the first organized athletic club at the University of Michigan?

55. Which Michigan athletic team won the most NCAA tournaments (since 1948)?

56. Who holds the record for the most goals in a hockey tournament game?

57. Which University of Michigan athletic team holds the record of 112 individual winners in a championship meet?

58. Match the baseball player with the professional teams he has played for:

Sports, Spirit and Fans — Questions

1) Charles Gehinger
2) John Herrnstein
3) Dave Campbell
4) Elliott Maddox
5) Bill Zepp
6) Bob Reed
7) Dick Wakefield
8) George Sisler

a) Detroit Tigers and Washington Senators
b) Detroit Tigers and San Diego Padres
c) Philadelphia Phillies
d) Detroit Tigers
e) Detroit Tigers
f) Minnesota Twins
g) Detroit Tigers
h) St. Louis Browns and Boston Braves

59. This 1947 education graduate was a football coach for the Chicago Bears. Who is he?

60. This former University of Michigan and University of Iowa football coach graduated in 1948. Who is he?

61. Leland S. MacPhail attended Michigan from 1907 to 1908 and was the president and treasurer of the New York _____.

62. Eli Zaret of the Class of 1972 is a sportscaster for _____ in Detroit.

63. Law graduate Branch Rickey '11 was president and general manager of the _____.

64. _____ was the first American to win a gold medal in the Greco-Roman wrestling competition of the 1984 Olympics.

Sports, Spirit and Fans — Questions

65. _____ played tight end for the University of Michigan and the Green Bay Packers and broadcasted Michigan football games.

66. Bill Freehan '66 was recruited by the Detroit Tigers in his _____ year.

67. Bruce Kimball, known as the "Comeback Kid" after surviving a serious accident, won which medal for diving in the 1984 Olympics?

68. _____ '78 won a bronze medal on the 1984 Olympic women's springboard team.

69. Rudy Tomjanovich played basketball for the Michigan Wolverines and then for the _____.

70. Hockey player _____ '62, M.B.A. '66, won three varsity letters while at Michigan. He set an NHL record for scoring six goals in one game, played hockey for the St. Louis Blues and the Detroit Redwings and is coach of the University hockey team.

71. Micki King Hogue was a _____ medalist in diving at the 1972 Olympics.

Sports, Spirit and Fans — Questions

72. The Medical Library was named in honor of this alumnus and owner of the Michigan Panthers. Name him.

73. Janet Guthrie '60 is the first woman race car driver to enter the _____.

74. Campy Russell played basketball for the Michigan Wolverines and the _____.

75. _____ is a sportscaster for ABC who covers college football, the Olympics and "The Wide World of Sports."

76. In 1975 this Wolverine football player threw an 83-yard pass, the longest in Wolverine history, to Jim Smith in a game against Purdue. He was a Big Ten batting champ and played baseball for the Detroit Tigers and the Toronto Blue Jays. Who is he?

77. Business graduate John L. Schroeder '68 is a professional _____.

78. This 1941 graduate received a Master of Arts in 1948 and is the University of Michigan athletic director. Who is he?

79. In 1875 a _____ club was organized on campus.

Sports, Spirit and Fans — Questions

80. The first University of Michigan baseball team (1866) was called the _____.
    a) Wolverines
    b) Maroons
    c) Maize and Blue
    d) Arbors

81. In 1869 the school mascot became the _____.

82. Who played the drum for the first University of Michigan band?

83. In what year was the first woman permitted to play in the concert band?

84. In 1858 the first musical organization was organized, containing fifteen students and called _____.

85. The University Musical Society, founded in 1880 by President Henry S. Frieze, closed with a festival of three concerts in 1893. This three-day event is still recognized by the University and called the _____.

86. What important contribution did the Waterman Gymnasium make in 1928 to the University of Michigan?

Sports, Spirit and Fans — Questions

87. In 1973, what were the first women's sports to gain official intercollegiate status?

88. What conference did the women's athletic teams join in 1981?

89. In 1981 and 1983, the first Big Ten titles for women were in what sports?

90. In whose name is an annual award given to the Michigan Woman Athlete of the Year?

91. What was one of the first sports enjoyed by University women?

92. What was presented to James M. Divuvale, captain of the University football team, in honor of the victory over Harvard University in 1930?

93. In 1873, who prevented the Michigan and Cornell football teams to play in Cleveland?

94. Who reached the 2,000-point mark in a basketball game against Iowa, January 17, 1981?

95. _____ of the 1912 U.S. Olympic Team took first place in the 100m dash and first place in the 200m dash.

Sports, Spirit and Fans — Questions

96. During the 1924 Olympics, James Brooken took second place in _____; Dehart Hubbard took first place in _____; and Eddie Tolan took first place in _____ and _____.

97. During the 1904, 1908 and 1912 Olympics, _____ took first place in the shot put competition.

98. John Garrets placed second in the 100m hurdles and third in the shot put during the _____ Olympics.

99. _____ of the 1904 U.S. Olympic Team placed first in the 60m, 100m and 200m dash.

100. What do Indian corn and lapis lazuli have in common with the University?

101. In 1859 the University Glee Club was the _____ college glee club to be organized in America.

102. This alumnus and former governor of New York was the business manager and soloist of the Glee Club. Who is he?

103. _____ '54 music graduate and member of the Glee Club, per-

formed as a tenor with the "Mitch Miller Show" and is a lead personality on "Sesame Street."

104. The 1959 Glee Club was the _____ American choir to win the male choir competition at Llangollen.

105. In September 1965 the Glee Club was one of five American choral groups to represent the United States at the first _____, held at Lincoln Center in New York and the National Cathedral in Washington, D.C.

106. What is the song of the University alma mater, and who was its author?

107. When was rugby introduced to the University of Michigan?

108. In 1947 the marching band made its first appearance at the _____ in Pasadena, California, conducted by Professor William Revelli, the founder and honorary life president of the College Board Directors National Association.

109. In 1951 the Glee Club, formed the first joint concert with what university?

110. The Glee Club performed their first

Sports, Spirit and Fans — Questions

four-week European Tour in 1955 and gave a special performance for Queen Juliana of _____.

111. Who was Alfred Eisenstaedt referring to in this 1950 **Life** Magazine quotation?
> It steps fastest and plays best of the college outfits that provide music and spectacle on football fields.

112. Which famous football coach designed the Michigan "winged" football helmet often used for recruiting purposes?

113. What prestigious award did the Michigan marching band receive in 1982?

114. Which University sophomore was the first Michigan baseball Olympian to win a silver medal in 1984?

115. Who served on the 1968 and 1972 Olympic track teams and was the first Michigander to make an Olympic track team?

116. What was the score of the October 1, 1898, opening football game between Michigan and Michigan Normal at Regents Field?

Sports, Spirit and Fans — Questions

117. What was the Wolverine football record in 1898?

118. For what performance is the University Choral Union and University Symphony Orchestra most noted?

119. From which Michigan song are these lines?
    > Garlands of blue bells and maize intertwine,
    > And hearts that are true and voices combine: Hail!

120. Who won the bronze medal in the steeplechase at the 1984 Los Angeles Olympics?

121. Steve Smith completed the most passes—118—during a football season. In what year?

122. Who won the September 30, 1950, opening football game between Michigan State and Michigan at Michigan Stadium?

123. Jack Clancy holds the record for _____ with 76 in 1966.

124. In 1978 Rich Leach had the most touchdown passes thrown during a season with _____ passes.

83

Sports, Spirit and Fans — Questions

125. Name the source of this statement: My days at the University of Michigan have always remained a highlight in my life because of the association of men and coaches with whom I played. I can think of no single happening which has contributed more to my good fortune and success in later life . . . .

126. Which Michigan football coach led his team to the most opening wins?

127. Which Michigan football coach had the least number of opening wins?

128. What was the score of the Michigan —Washington State opening game held at Michigan Stadium September 10, 1983?

129. Which former Michigan Regent and 1958 Law School graduate captained the 1955 Michigan Big Ten Championship tennis team?

130. In 1982 _____ had the most yards gained in a season with 1,735 yards.

131. What was the score of the Michigan Wolverines—Michigan State Spartans opening game at Michigan Stadium October 6, 1934?

Sports, Spirit and Fans — Questions

132. Which player holds the record for total offense with 6,554 yards?

133. What player scored the most points —117—in a season (in 1940)?

134. On what date did Fielding Yost coach his first football game at Regents Field? What was the score of the game?

135. What was the score of the opening football game between Michigan and Ohio Wesleyan at Regents Field on September 30, 1905?

136. What player scored the most touchdowns in a season (in 1968)?

137. In 1980 _____ had the most touchdown passes in a season, with 14 to his credit.

138. Who won the opening Michigan versus Missouri football game at Michigan Stadium?

139. What was the Wolverine football record in 1901, and what did they accomplish?

140. Bo Schembechler made his first appearance as head football coach at Michigan Stadium September 20, 1969, when Michigan beat _____, 42-14.

Sports, Spirit and Fans — Questions

141. What was the score of the opening football game between Michigan and Illinois at Michigan Stadium on September 16, 1978?

142. What player holds the total offense season record for his performance in 1981?

143. What was the score of the opening game between Michigan and Great Lakes at Michigan Stadium on September 15, 1945?

144. Where was the opening football game held when Michigan beat California 41-0 on September 28, 1940?

145. Which football player had the most net yards gained in rushing in a season (in 1976)?

146. Michigan beat Air Force on September 26, 1964, at the Michigan Stadium and went on to win the conference championship. What was the score of that game?

147. On September 28, 1957, Michigan beat Southern California 16-6. Where was this game held?

148. What player holds the records for most passes completed—324—

Sports, Spirit and Fans — Questions

and most yards gained—4,860—in a season?

149. Butch Woolfolk '81 has the highest career record in rushing with ____ yards.

150. This 1982 graduate caught the most passes—161—and the most touchdown passes—37—during a career. Who is he?

151. Fill in the missing words of "The Victors," by Louis Elbel:
    Hail! to the victors valiant
    Hail! to the conquering heroes
    Hail! Hail! to Michigan, the leaders and best
    Hail! to the victors valiant
    Hail! to the conquering heroes,
    Hail! Hail! to Michigan the ____.

152. What cartoon character is often personified by Michigan students at football games?

ANSWERS

1. Approximately 120,000

2. Approximately 30,000

3. d) The Glee Club. Butterfield Theatres Inc. presented an RKO-Pathé Audio Motion Picture entitled "Here Comes the Band," which featured the University of Michigan Varsity Glee Club and the Midnite Sons Quartette. The film opens with "Yellow and Blue," "The Victors" and "Cossack," and finishes with a medley of old Michigan songs.

4. Washington's Birthday Celebration (February 22, 1887)

Sports, Spirit and Fans — Answers

5. d) All of the above

6. 23,726,116

7. 349

8. November 17, 1979, an NCAA attendance record was set with 106,155 fans watching the University of Michigan—Ohio State game.

9. 730,315

10. d) 90,286

11. a) Ohio State

12. a) Eleven

13. Stanford University

14. b) Minnesota

15. Orange (Oklahoma 14, Michigan 6)

16. North Carolina (North Carolina 17, Michigan 15)

17. Holiday (Brigham Young 24, Michigan 15)

18. 1981 (Michigan 33, UCLA 14)

19. Auburn (Auburn 9, Michigan 7)

Sports, Spirit and Fans — Answers

20. Nebraska. Michigan won, 27-23. With 72,454 people in attendance, it was considered the largest Fiesta Bowl crowd ever.

21. Jim Harbaugh, #4

22. Bo Schembechler, on "NBC Sports," January 1, 1986

23. Three wins, ten losses

24. Ohio State

25. 1) e
    2) d
    3) a
    4) c
    5) b

26. 100,000

27. During the fall of 1897, the University of Michigan went to Detroit, with a score of Michigan 14, Minnesota 0.

28. Tom Harmon, Michigan's Heisman Trophy winner and All-American halfback (1939-1940)

29. He wore forty-seven jerseys during his 1938-1940 football career.

30. Mark Harmon

Sports, Spirit and Fans — Answers

31. d) All of the above. Francis Wistert '33, Albert Wistert '42 and Alvin Wistert 1948-49, were all tackles.

32. During the period from 1901 to 1905, 2,821 points were scored in 57 games for a 49.5 scoring average. In 50 games, Michigan shut out the opposition and the following victories were achieved: 128-0 over Buffalo in 1901; 119-0 over Michigan State in 1901; 107-0 over Iowa in 1902; and 130-0 over West Virginia in 1904.

33. Elroy "Crazy Legs" Hirsch

34. 27 winning team titles and 179 individual titles

35. Ruth Pickett '81

36. True

37. 1956

38. 100m backstroke

39. Springboard diving

40. Bruce Harlan

41. Breaststroke

42. Fielding H. Yost, head football

Sports, Spirit and Fans — Answers

coach (1901-1926) and University of Michigan athletic director

43. The "Little Brown Jug" was a token jug that was presented to the winner of the Michigan—Minnesota football games. Fielding H. Yost was the recipient.

44. Adolph Germany Schulz played football from 1904 to 1908. He was placed on the All-Time Football Team by the Associated Press in 1951 and by the Football Writers of America in 1969.

45. Willie Heston, LL.B. '04

46. Ted Sizemore '66

47. Hatch was the group manager of the football team from 1921 to 1964 who helped to determine the ownership of the jug.

48. Bennie Oosterbaan

49. Herbert O. "Fritz" Crisler

50. Coach Cliff Keen

51. c) 1963 and 1970

52. Marty Bodnak

Sports, Spirit and Fans — Answers

53. "Two uprights with a cross-beam and ropes dangling from eye-bolts, the remains of some prehistoric effort toward muscular development" —what passed for a gymnasium.

54. In 1865 fifty dollars was set aside by the regents for the Pioneer Cricket Club, of which there were twenty-five members.

55. The Michigan hockey team won seven tournaments and tied with Boston University for a total of thirteen tournament appearances.

56. Gil Burford '51 of Michigan holds an individual record of five goals.

57. The swim team

58. 1) d
    2) c
    3) b
    4) a
    5) f
    6) e
    7) g
    8) h

59. George Allen

60. Chalmers "Bump" Elliott

61. Yankees

Sports, Spirit and Fans — Answers

62. WDIV

63. Dodgers

64. Steve Fraser, M.P.A. '63

65. Ron Kramer '57

66. Sophomore

67. Silver

68. Chris Seufert

69. Houston Rockets

70. Red Berenson

71. Gold

72. Alfred Taubman, 1945-1948

73. Indianapolis 500

74. Cleveland Cavaliers

75. Bill Fleming

76. Rick Leach

77. Golpher

78. Don Canham

79. Boating

Sports, Spirit and Fans — Answers

80. b) Maroons

81. Wolverine

82. Irving K. Pond 1879

83. 1932

84. Les Sans Souci

85. May Festival

86. It was the first intramural sports building in America and the place where "paddleball" was invented by Earl Kiskey.

87. Basketball, field hockey, volleyball, tennis and swimming

88. The Big Ten Conference

89. Volleyball, gymnastics and indoor track

90. Marie Hartwig, the prime developer of women's athletics at the University

91. Baseball

92. A spike, handmade in the workshop of Paul Revere, used in the original construction of the USS Constitution ("Old Ironsides")

Sports, Spirit and Fans — Answers

93. Andrew Dickson White, Michigan alumnus and president of Cornell University, stated: "I will not permit thirty men to travel four hundred miles merely to agitate a bag of wind."

94. Mike McGee, All-American #40

95. Ralph Craig

96. The pole vault; the broad jump; 100m dash and 200m dash

97. Ralph Rose, 1945-1947

98. 1908

99. Archie Hahn, LL.B. '04

100. In 1867, Indian corn, or maize, and lapis lazuli, or blue, were chosen as the University of Michigan colors.

101. Second

102. Thomas E. Dewey

103. Robert McGrath

104. First

105. International University Choral Festival

Sports, Spirit and Fans — Answers

106. "The Yellow and Blue" was written by Charles M. Gayley 1878, LL.D. '04, and professor of Latin (1880-1886).

107. 1876

108. Rose Bowl

109. Cornell

110. The Netherlands

111. The Michigan Band

112. Fritz Crisler, in 1938

113. The John Philip Sousa Foundation awarded the Sudler Trophy to the Michigan band.

114. Barry Larkin

115. Francie Kraker Goodridge

116. Michigan 21, Michigan Normal 0

117. 10-0

118. Handel's **Messiah** is performed every December in Hill Auditorium.

119. "The Yellow and Blue"

Sports, Spirit and Fans — Answers

120. Brian Diemer '83

121. 1982

122. Michigan State, 14-7

123. Pass receptions per season

124. Seventeen

125. Tom Harmon, 1940 Heisman Trophy winner, in the September 8, 1984, official football program

126. Fielding Yost, with 24

127. Harry Kipke, with 5

128. Michigan 20, Washington State 17

129. Robert E. Nederlander

130. Steve Smith

131. Michigan State 16, Michigan 0

132. Steve Smith '83

133. Tom Harmon

134. September 28, 1901; Michigan 50, Albion 0

135. Michigan 65, Ohio Wesleyan 0

136. Ron Johnson, with 19 touchdowns

Sports, Spirit and Fans — Answers

137. Anthony Carter

138. Michigan, 42-7

139. The Wolverines completed the 1901 season with an 11-0 record and won the first Rose Bowl Game, the conference title, and the national championship.

140. Vanderbilt

141. Michigan 31, Illinois 0

142. Steve Smith '83, with 2,335 yards

143. Michigan 27, Great Lakes 2

144. Berkeley Memorial Stadium

145. Rob Lytle, with 1,469 yards

146. Michigan 24, Air Force 7

147. Los Angeles Colosseum

148. Steve Smith '83

149. 3,861

150. Anthony Carter

151. "Champions of the West"

152. Bullwinkle

THE WOLVERINES

1. A wolverine is all of the following items except:
   a) the University of Michigan mascot and team name.
   b) the largest member of the weasel family.
   c) the state animal of Michigan.
   d) a carnivore.
   e) a nocturnal animal.
   f) a University of Michigan student.

2. Which Ann Arbor restaurant, located at 1201 South University, was also known by the following titles?
   — The White Helmet Restaurant (1928)

The Wolverines — Questions

- The Shack Restaurant (1929-1930)
- Lincoln Restaurant (1931)
- Essex Restaurant (1932-1934)
- Essex House Jas Argereu (1935)
- McDonald Dairy Store (1936)

3. Which of the following people is noted for giving lectures during the 1960s and 1970s in the Diag?
   a) "Shaky Jake"
   b) "Doctor Diag"
   c) Filibert "Daddy" Roth
   d) All of the above

4. In 1904, what campus event was billed as "unsurpassed by any college function in the United States" and the "Michigan Crowning Social Event"?

5. In 1868 _____ was worn by one-fourth of the literary department for one year and then abandoned.

6. What did the Class of 1868 hold the evening before Thanksgiving Day, 1968?

7. What was the name of the first student publication, begun in 1853?

The Wolverines — Questions

8. What was the name of the weekly college paper in 1866?

9. In 1867 the two publications above joined to form the _____.

10. In 1868 a group of students known as the _____ made holes in the floor of the president's room in the Law Building in order to listen to the faculty from the basement below.

11. In 1856 a dispute between two students and the proprietor of a German saloon, Herr Hangsterfer's, was known as the _____.

12. What event was known as "Cap Night?"

13. What was the "swing-out" ceremony?

14. Which of the following did seniors carry during the month of May from 1869 until 1930?
    a) Beer
    b) Canes
    c) Michigan jackets
    d) Yearbooks

15. Which class was the first to wear academic gowns at commencement?

The Wolverines — Questions

16. In 1906 the freshmen class challenged the sixty-member sophomore class to what event?

17. What tradition was known as the "Great Rock Scrap"?

18. Who was "Skeezer," and what important contribution did he make to the University of Michigan?

19. According to the **Guiness Book of College Records and Facts**, what campus-wide game was developed at the University of Michigan?

20. Which of the following bars were student hangouts in the late 1800s?
    a) The Orient
    b) Rick's American Cafe
    c) Chuubs
    d) Goodtime Charlie's
    e) Hangsterfer's
    f) Bennigans
    g) Bicycle Club
    h) Binders
    i) Ashleys
    j) Apostle's Club
    k) The Brown Jug
    l) Pretzel Bell
    m) Dooley's
    n) Prettyman's
    o) Bimbo's
    p) Joe Parker's
    q) Tangerine Ballroom

21. Two of these bars are noted in the lyrics of the song "I Want to Go Back to Michigan." Which bars are they? Where were they located?

22. In Aaron Spelling's film **Mr. Mom**, directed by Stan Dragoti, which actress wears a Michigan sweatshirt?

103

The Wolverines — Questions

23. Which noted English Shakespearean actor appeared at Hill Auditorium on Tuesday, October 21, 1958?

24. Which famous silent movie actress made her first appearance on a lecture platform in Hill Auditorium on November 30, 1944?

25. On February 10, 1958, at Hill Auditorium, two United States senators debated the question: "Is our foreign policy sound?" Who were these senators?

26. The 1930 Nobel Prize winner in Literature and author of **It Can't Happen Here**, **Main Street** and **Dodsworth** debated "Democracies Chance to Survive" with author Lewis Browne, December 2, 1941, in Hill Auditorium. Who is this author?

27. This Academy Award-winning actor starred in **Rembrandt**, **Mutiny on the Bounty** and **Henry VIII**, and lectured at Hill Auditorium on February 19, 1951. Who is he?

28. _____ served as United States treasurer under President Dwight D. Eisenhower and was active in improving the advancement

The Wolverines — Questions

of women in government. She spoke November 13, 1956, at Hill Auditorium.

29. A famous social activist and wife of a U.S. president introduced International Week, November 18, 1958, before an audience of six thousand in Hill Auditorium. She spoke on the topic, "Is America Facing World Leadership?" Who is she?

30. What do Tom Berenger, Glenn Close, Jeff Goldblum, William Hurt, Kevin Kline, Mary Kay Place and JoBeth Williams have in common with the University of Michigan?

31. In **The Big Chill**, which character, although a "brilliant physics student at the University of Michigan, paradoxically chose to turn his back on science and taste of life through a seemingly random series of occupations"?

32. Which **Big Chill** character graduates from the University of Michigan and wins the leading role in the action-filled detective television series "J.T. Lancer"? Which actor portrayed this character?

105

The Wolverines — Questions

33. Nick entered the doctoral program in psychology at the University of Michigan in 1972 and later became a radio psychologist. Which Academy Award-winning actor played this character in **The Big Chill**?

34. For which of the following magazines does the character Michael, played by Jeff Goldblum, work?
    a) **Time**
    b) **GQ**
    c) **Esquire**
    d) **People**

35. Harold and Sara Cooper, played by Kevin Kline and Glenn Close, host the Michigan reunion and are the only pair who married. With whom did Sara have a "love affair since Ann Arbor"?

36. What other couple considers marriage in this film?

37. Which of the following roles did alumnus Lawrence Kasdan have in this film?
    a) Executive producer
    b) Writer
    c) Actor
    d) Director

The Wolverines — Questions

38. Which two characters planned to buy "land near Saginow, Michigan" during their senior year at the University of Michigan?

39. During the film, the characters watch a University of Michigan football game.
    1) Who are the Wolverines playing?
    2) What is the score?
    3) Who is the coach?

40. Name the character who states, "Come on Bo, you are not supposed to fold until the fourth quarter."

41. In which of the following places was **The Big Chill** filmed?
    a) Ann Arbor, Michigan
    b) Grand Rapids, Michigan
    c) Columbus, Ohio
    d) Beaufort, South Carolina and Atlanta, Georgia

42. Which of the following lines were spoken in **The Big Chill**?
    a) "Neither time nor distance could break the bonds that we feel."
    b) "I feel I was at my best when I was with you people."
    c) "When I lost touch with this group, I lost my idea of what I should be."

The Wolverines — Questions

    d) "If I hear 'Heard It Through the Grapevine' one more time, I'm going to slit my own wrists."
    e) All of the above

43. The administration of 1844 suspended students for belonging to the Chi Psi and Beta Theta Pi fraternities. Members of one fraternity, however, were allowed to remain in their organization if they signed the following document, known as the code of 1847:
> Resolved, that no student shall be admitted into any class without examination satisfactory to the faculty and giving a pledge that he will not be a member of any society, which is not approved by the faculty.

    Which fraternity signed these words?

44. What was the first University sorority?

45. What was the first structure ever to be built by an American college fraternity?

46. Who did the 1848 faculty call a "detail of obliquities" and guilty of "debauchery, drunkenness and pugilism"?

The Wolverines — Questions

47. The first fraternity house constructed in Ann Arbor was for _____ in 1880, and was located _____.

48. Where was Alpha Delta Phi originally located, from 1875 to 1876?

49. What was the first professional fraternity established at the University?

50. Which fraternity and sorority were first chartered at the University of Michigan?

51. According to Robert Egan's **From Here to Fraternity**, how did former President Gerald Ford pay his way through school?

52. Which two fraternities traditionally take part in the Mud Bowl?

53. When the office of the University's literary magazine, **The Inlander**, closed in the fall of 1919 to serve the interest of the students returning from World War I, what did Stellanova Brunt Osborn '22, M.A. '30, Litt.D. '78, do?

54. When Osborn complained to President Marion Leroy Burton that creative writing was not encour-

The Wolverines — Questions

aged on the campus, who was chosen to be the University's poet-in-residence for a salary of five thousand dollars?

55. In 1922, what other poets visited the Ann Arbor campus to present lectures?

56. Before student Mike Wallace discovered his love for the University broadcast center, what careers had he originally intended to pursue as a freshman?

57. Who was Mike Wallace's studio engineer at the University broadcast center?

58. According to Vicki Goldberg's biography, which famous photographer notes in her diary that as a University student she was almost locked in a fourth-floor men's toilet overnight and once climbed a rope to the engineering building's roof in order to get a picture of the University's clock tower?

59. Name the source of this passage: "Well, she'd find out when she got to Michigan. If there was that same dream feeling about Michigan, then Francie would know that she was the one dreaming. Ann Arbor!"

ANSWERS

1. c) The State Animal of Michigan

2. The Brown Jug (since 1938)

3. b) "Doctor Diag"

4. The fraternity-sponsored Junior Hop, held in the Waterman Gymnasium, was sponsored during the close of examination week on the evening before the second semester. Begun in 1883, this tradition was followed by a University of Michigan Glee Club concert and sleigh rides.

5. The Oxford cap. It was blue and had a square top, a black tassel and a moveable "U of M" visor.

6. The Senior Hop

The Wolverines — Answers

7. **University Magazine**

8. **The University Chronicle**

9. **Chronicle**

10. "Lower House Faculty"

11. Dutch War

12. Members of the freshmen class wore caps called "pots." At the end of the year students were led in procession by the varsity band to a ceremony at the Sleepy Hollow gully, where they threw these flannel caps into a burning "M" bonfire on the hillside, thus symbolizing their liberation from freshmen year. Following speeches and songs, "M" blankets were given to seniors with athletic letters. Cap Night was first celebrated Saturday, June 11, 1904, and continued on the first Saturday night of June. This practice was discontinued in 1934.

13. The swing-out ceremony marked the first Wednesday that the graduating class wore their caps and gowns. This practice was discontinued in 1934.

14. b) Canes

The Wolverines — Answers

15. The Class of 1894

16. A tug of war. With a flag placed in the center of a 350-foot rope, teams of students pulled their opponents across the river.

17. In 1906 freshmen painted their class numbers on a large boulder and placed it on the campus grounds. The sophomores would then try to steal this boulder.

18. "Skeezer" was a dog who worked as a canine therapist at the UM Children's Psychiatric Hospital.

19. "Killer." This game was inspired in 1965 by the Carlo Ponti film **The Tenth Victim**. The object of the game is to search for other students and "shoot" them with rubber-tipped darts. A winner is determined when all other players have been eliminated. Some students felt this game was a fun way for freshmen students to get acquainted.

20. a) Orient   j) Apostle's Club
    c) Chuubs   n) Prettyman's
    e) Hangsterfer's p) Joe Parker's
    h) Binders

21. Orient and Joe Parkers:
    "I want to go back to Michigan
    To dear Ann Arbor town.

The Wolverines — Answers

Back to **Joe's** and the **Orient**...." The Orient was located on Main Street and "Joe's" on Huron Street.

22. Teri Garr

23. Sir John Gielgud

24. Lillian Gish

25. Hubert Humphrey and Thruston B. Morton

26. Sinclair Lewis

27. Charles Laughton

28. Ivy Baker Priest

29. Eleanor Roosevelt

30. They all starred in **The Big Chill**, a film about the reunion of a group of University of Michigan graduates.

31. Alex Marshall

32. Sam Weber, played by Tom Berenger

33. William Hurt

34. d) **People**

The Wolverines — Answers

35. Alex Marshall

36. Sam and Karen, portrayed by Tom Berenger and JoBeth Williams

37. a, b and d

38. Harold and Michael, played by Kevin Kline and Jeff Goldblum

39.
    1) Michigan State
    2) Michigan 10, Michigan State 0
    3) Bo Schembechler

40. Michael

41. d) Beaufort, South Carolina, and Atlanta, Georgia

42. e) a, b and c

43. Alpha Delta Phi

44. Kappa Alpha Theta (1879)

45. The Chi Psi chapter house, in a cabin in the woods east of the campus near the Forest Hill Cemetery

46. Fraternities

47. Psi Upsilon; on the corner of State Street and South University

48. The site where Hill Auditorium is located

The Wolverines — Answers

49. Phi Delta Phi law fraternity, established 1869

50. Acacia fraternity, May 12, 1904, and Theta Phi Alpha sorority, August 30, 1912

51. Ford worked as a dishwasher at Delta Kappa Epsilon.

52. Sigma Alpha Epsilon and Phi Delta Theta

53. Osborn began the first edition of **Whimsies**, an underground creative writing magazine, with the aid of four other women.

54. Robert Frost

55. Carl Sandburg, Padraic Colum, Amy Lowell, Louis Untermeyer, Jean Starr Untermeyer and Vachel Lindsay

56. Teaching or law

57. Jerome Wiesner '37, M.S. '38, Ph.D. '50, president of MIT from 1971 to 1980

58. Margaret Bourke-White, 1922-1924

59. **A Tree Grows in Brooklyn**, by Betty Smith

CAMPUS TOUR GUIDE

1. Since the administration of Dr. Henry Phillip Tappan, all presidents have lived in this home except one. Who is he? Where did he live? Who lived here in his place?

2. True or False: This structure is the oldest building on the University of Michigan campus.

3. What did President James B. Angell insist be installed in this building?

4. What happened to the three other buildings of similar classical revival architecture?

5. What purpose did the President's House serve from 1916 until 1920?

6. In 1970 the President's House was the first structure in Ann Arbor to be _____.

Campus Tour Guide — Questions

7. Where is this sculpture located?

8. What type of animal does this sculpture represent?

9. Why was this particular animal selected?

10. What was the position of the person for whom the building behind the sculpture is named?

11. A _____ is located on the fourth floor of this building.

12. For what reason did this building have a record high of 17,235 visitors in March 1971?

13. What inscription is found at the top of this building?

14. In 1929 an anonymous donation was made of a collection of native Michigan animals, which lived behind this building in a round house for thirty-four years. What happened to these badgers, bobcats, porcupines, skunks, red foxes, black bears, raccoons, wolverines, otters, snakes and amphibians?

Campus Tour Guide — Questions

15. This structure, known as the University Observatory, was constructed in 1854 under the administration of President Tappan. What was it originally called?

16. True or False: The Observatory contains the first large telescope ever constructed at a university and the _____ largest lens in the world.

Campus Tour Guide — Questions

17. What is the name of this structure?

18. Which group of people were not allowed access to this building until 1954?

19. Whose home originally stood at the site of this building?

20. Who was the founder of this building?

21. The U Club, located within this structure, is now a terrace and dining room facility; but in December 1911, the Club was started as an organization for _____.
    a) fencing and boxing c) band practice
    b) honors society   d) alumni meetings

22. True or False: This building is called "the home of campus life for present, past and future students of the University of Michigan as a unifying force in the life of its students, alumni, faculty, staff and friends."

Campus Tour Guide — Questions

23. This building is named after the Latin professor who served as acting president following the unexpected resignation of Erastus Haven, introduced coeducation to the University, and promoted the Choral Union and University Musical Society. What is the name of this structure?

24. The Social Work, Communication, Theatre and Near Eastern Studies Departments are located in this building. From 1905 to 1956, however, it served a different purpose. What was its function?

Campus Tour Guide — Questions

25. The President's House, the University Observatory and this building are listed in the National Park Science Register of Historical Places. What is the name of this structure?

26. Late 19th-century German _____ designed this Romanesque-styled structure.

27. Who was the first occupant of this building?

28. In 1924 the first UM fieldwork in archaeology was done in the _____.

29. What was the original name of this building?

30. The circular tower at the top of this building was designed by which famous Boston architect?

Campus Tour Guide — Questions

31. In order to build this structure, thirty-two buildings on two city blocks had to be removed before construction could begin. What is the name of this building?

32. For which group of students was this building primarily designed?

Campus Tour Guide — Questions

33. The carillon, clock and tower on the University of Michigan campus was dedicated on December 4, 1936, to President Marion Leroy _____.

34. The bell tower is designed to symbolize the idealism of university life in the course of _____.

Campus Tour Guide — Questions

35. In 1935 Charles M. Baird, of Kansas City, Missouri, donated the funds to build the bell tower. Baird was the former _____ director of the University.

36. On the tenth floor of the bell tower is the sixty-seven-bell carillon. The one-hundred-ton Baird Carillon is the _____ heaviest musical instrument in the world.
    a) third
    b) tenth
    c) twentieth
    d) none of the above

37. The smallest bell in the Baird Carillon weighs forty-one pounds, while the largest bell, "Big Baird," weighs _____ tons.

Campus Tour Guide — Questions

38. On May 12, 1929, this bench was erected on the twenty-fifth anniversary of the founding of the national council of this fraternity. What is the name of the council?

39. When was this fraternity founded?

40. What tradition did this chapter start at the UM?

41. To be considered for membership during the first twenty-nine years of this fraternity, a student was required to be a _____.

Campus Tour Guide — Questions

42. What is the name of this 2,400-pound painted steel sculpture which spins diagonally on its axis when pushed?

43. To whom was this sculpture dedicated?

44. Who donated this cube to the University of Michigan?

45. Where is this sculpture located?

Campus Tour Guide — Questions

46. This ten-by-thirty-foot steel sculpture contains five parallelograms. Name the sculpture.

47. This sculpture sits in front of a building that was designed by alumni for alumni, and dedicated to alumni May 11, 1910—but is not used for alumni. What is the name of the building?

48. In 1950 Dr. and Mrs. Walter R. Parker of Grosse Pointe, Michigan, donated the artwork of James Abbott McNeill _____ to this building.

49. What is the name of this glass hallway that connects Mason and Haven Halls?

50. Haven Hall replaced Old Haven Hall. What did Mason Hall replace?

51. After whom is Mason Hall named?

52. True or False: Mason Hall, completed in 1841, was the second University building used to house students.

53. Old Haven Hall served the University of Michigan from 1863 to 1950. For which of the following purposes was it used?
    a) Law school (for sixty years)
    b) Chapel (1973)
    c) Library (1883)
    d) Regent meeting place
    e) All of the above

54. What happened to Old Haven Hall?

Campus Tour Guide — Questions

55. Which of the following campus buildings contains these architectural columns and fragments, including the Doric entrance from the First National Bank of Michigan, erected in Detroit, 1836, and the entrance of the old Detroit Post Office building, 1931?
    a) Lorch Hall
    b) Michigan Union
    c) Museum of Art
    d) Kelsey Museum of Archaeology

56. Why are these columns here?

57. Which University of Michigan building temporarily existed in this garden and was featured in 1954 in **Life** Magazine?

Campus Tour Guide — Questions

58. The names of Carolus Fox, Professor of Agriculture, Samuel Denton, Professor of Medicine, Joseph Whiting, Evangelii Minister, and Douglas Houghton, M.D., Professor of Chemistry and Geology, are inscribed on this white stone pole next to what building?

59. This library contains frescoes by Gari Melchers called **The Arts of War** and **The Arts of Peace**. These were painted in 1893 for the Manufacturer's Building at what event?

Campus Tour Guide — Questions

60. What is the name of this building?

61. For whom is this structure named?

62. What words are inscribed in bas relief over the main door?

63. What sentence is carved in stone over the facade?

Campus Tour Guide — Questions

64. The inscription on this rock reads:
   This rock and the elm beside it were placed here in 1869 as a memorial by the class of that year.
   In front of which building is this rock located?

133

Campus Tour Guide — Questions

65. This building was designed by Albert Kahn, Inc., of Detroit, the designer of the automobile plants, Angell Hall, the East Medical Building and East Engineering, and the winner of the 1972 Honors Award of the Detroit Chapter of the American Institute of Architects. What is the name of this structure?

Campus Tour Guide — Questions

66. This structure contains a letter from Christopher Columbus to Queen Isabella, dated 1493, describing the New World. What is the name of this building?

67. The following inscriptions are located on the facade of this structure:
    > In darkness dwells the people which know its annals not.
    >
    > Tradition fades but the written record remains ever fresh.

    Who wrote these words?

68. What is the name of the structure behind this building?

Campus Tour Guide — Questions

69. Where are these two concrete books located?

70. Who was "Beal"?

Campus Tour Guide — Questions

71. What is the name of this stainless-steel sculpture?

72. Where is this structure located?

73. How many pounds do each of the triangles weigh?

74. Who is the sculptor?

Campus Tour Guide — Questions

75. In 1906 Professor Walter H. Nichols 1891 and Esther Connor Nichols 1894 gave the University of Michigan twenty-seven acres of land between Geddes Avenue and the Huron River after unsuccessfully growing fruit and vegetables on its hills. This land is called "The Nichols Arboretum" or the _____.

Campus Tour Guide — Questions

76. In front of which building is this sculpture located?

77. What is the nickname of this sculpture?

78. From an aerial view, this building is said to look like a _____.

79. This corner was named in honor of alumni Lt. Col. James A. McDivitt and Lt. Col. Edward H. White after they returned to the University of Michigan from their space mission on the _____.

80. During their visit at the University of Michigan, McDivitt and White dedicated what honorary degree?

Campus Tour Guide — Questions

81. Name this building, which contains a 1,420-seat theater for drama, dance and concerts.

82. Regent Emeritus Eugene B. Power donated _____ dollars to build this center.

83. A tapestry by which famous artist hangs in the lobby?

Campus Tour Guide — Questions

Campus Tour Guide — Questions

84. These three building are all part of the Law Quadrangle donated by whom?

85. The Law Quad is the first "_____ law school in America."

86. The donator of the Law Quad insisted on waiting to see his gift, the largest ever received by the University, upon completion. This never happened—why?

87. What does the Law Quad have in common with Oxford and Cambridge?

Campus Tour Guide — Questions

88. This site appears to be a long sidewalk that criss-crosses behind the Harlan Hatcher Graduate Library. It is, however, the focus of political and social rallies, demonstrations, protests and campaign speeches. This active spot has witnessed Martin Luther King Day celebrations, South African apartheid protests, Walter Mondale and Gary Hart campaign speeches and an interview by NBC's **Today Show** host Bryant Gumbel with President Harold T. Shapiro. This site of progressive happenings is known as the _____.

Campus Tour Guide — Questions

89. This structure was also contributed by the donor of the Law Quadrangle in honor of his mother. What is the name of this building?

90. This all women's residence was originally designed in 1915 for what purpose?

Campus Tour Guide — Questions

91. Why was Levi Barbour inspired to donate this gift?

92. Who was Betsy Barbour?

Campus Tour Guide — Questions

93. What is the legend of this bronze seal?

94. Where is this located?

95. Which class donated the seal?

147

Campus Tour Guide — Questions

Courtesy the UM Athletic Department

96. Michigan Stadium, with a seating capacity of 101,701 people, is the largest college-owned structure. The Stadium was originally built in 1927 for $950,000 with the ability to seat _____ spectators.

97. Against what team was the first game played in the newly designed stadium, October 1, 1927? Who won?

98. In 1949 steel stands replaced the old wooden bleachers, which raised the seating to:
    a) 85,000.
    b) 84,401.
    c) 87,000.
    d) 97,329.

99. True or False: Seating capacity was raised to 101,001 in 1965.

Campus Tour Guide — Questions

Courtesy the UM Athletic Department

100. Fourteen thousand spectators watch University basketball games, concerts, and gymnastic and wrestling events in the _____.

101. After whom was this structure named?

Campus Tour Guide — Questions

Courtesy the Bentley Historical Library

102. "Here at 2:00 a.m. on October 14, 1960, John Fitzgerald Kennedy first defined the _____. He stood at the place marked by the medallion and was cheered by a large and enthusiastic student audience for the hope and promise his idea gave the world."

103. In front of which University building is JFK standing?

Campus Tour Guide — Questions

Courtesy the Bentley Historical Library

104. This graduate of the Class of 1949 starred as Alice in a hit television series where she worked to keep the "Bunch" together. Who is she? (photo from the Michiganensian Yearbook)

Courtesy the UM Athletic Department

105. Which prominent magazine, dated December 11, 1939, featured the University of Michigan cheerleading squad?

106. Alumnus Andrew Mowbray Ritter developed the _____, or the Grand Salaam, in which the cheerleader twists into an arc while in a back flip and lands straight up on the ground.

Courtesy the Bentley Historical Library

107. Who is this person?

108. He served the University from June 28, 1871, to October 1, 1909, but his administration was interrupted on four separate occasions. What were these events?

109. Why did he resign at the age of eighty, not at seventy-six as intended?

153

110. At what special holiday celebration was the first public appearance of the University of Michigan band?

111. What was the first football game attended by the Michigan band?

112. Who wrote "The Victors"?

Campus Tour Guide — Questions

113. Who is the woman in the center of the picture?

114. What important contribution did she make to the University?

155

Courtesy the UM Athletic Department

115. What position did Anthony Carter play on the University football team?

116. What special recognitions did Carter receive in NCAA history?

117. For what professional team did Carter play?

Campus Tour Guide — Questions

118. This event, held the first three weeks in July, encompasses art, theater, music and dance on the University grounds. What is the event?

Courtesy the UM Athletic Department

119. Who is this person?

120. During the Michigan—Michigan State game, October 6, 1979, he helped Michigan win its _____ victory.

121. In 1969 he was given what honor?

158

Campus Tour Guide — Questions

Courtesy the Ben... ...torical Library

122. What is the name of this traditional University ceremony?

123. Which group of people participated?

124. What specific traditions were practiced during this event?

Campus Tour Guide — Questions

125. Who is football player #48?

126. What position did he play for the University?

127. Of which fraternity was he a member?

128. While in office, this person replaced "Hail to the Chief" with what song?

Campus Tour Guide — Questions

129. What is the name of this building?

130. Which graduating class met and formed the first Society of Alumni group?

131. What is the second oldest and first monthly alumni publication in the United States?

161

ANSWERS

1. As former dean of the law school, President Harry Burns Hutchins chose to remain in his own home on Monroe Street. President Angell lived out the remainder of his life in this home.

2. True

3. The first indoor plumbing in Ann Arbor was installed in 1871.

4. Four houses were designed to house the faculty. In 1840 two homes were constructed on either side of the campus, of which only the present day President's Home remains. The three other original

homes were torn down to make room for the Clements Library and the Chemistry and Natural Science Buildings.

5. The President's Home served as a Red Cross Station during World War I.

6. entered in the National Register of Historic Places

7. In front of the Alexander G. Ruthven Museum Building

8. A puma

9. The puma was chosen symbolically as a representation of energy and respect, and aesthetically because it would not detract from the museum's design. The puma is a Michigan native in danger of extinction.

10. Ruthven was the seventh president of the University of Michigan.

11. planetarium

12. A twelve-day display of the Apollo XII moon rock

13. "Go to nature; take the facts into your own hands; look and see for yourself."

Campus Tour Guide — Answers

14. In 1963 the animal house was torn down to build a new research wing. The director of the Ruthven Museum received 250 requests for the animals.

15. The Detroit Observatory

16. third

17. The Union

18. Women

19. Judge Thomas M. Cooley

20. Edward F. Parker '04

21. a) fencing and boxing

22. True

23. The Henry Simmons Frieze Building

24. The Frieze Building was originally the Ann Arbor High School.

25. The Kelsey Museum of Archaeology, named after the professor of Latin language and literature (1899-1927)

26. stone masons

Campus Tour Guide — Answers

27. The Student Christian Association

28. Near East

29. Newberry Hall, after John Newberry, the husband of Helen Newberry

30. H.H. Richardson

31. The Rackham Building

32. Graduate students

33. Burton

34. "humanity and civilization"

35. athletic

36. a) third

37. 12¼

38. Acacia, the only national fraternity to use a Greek word for a name. "Acacia" is the English translation of the Greek word for "everlasting."

39. May 12, 1904

40. "Night on the Nile" parties, with a fraternity-built Sphinx or pyramid

Campus Tour Guide — Answers

41. mason

42. Regents Plaza Rosenthal Cube

43. In June 1969 this sculpture was dedicated to the men and women who had served as regents at the University.

44. Sculptor and Michigan alumnus Bernard Rosenthal and the Class of 1965

45. The Regents Plaza Rosenthal Cube is located between the LSA Building and the Student Activities Building.

46. "Daedalus," installed September 1977

47. Alumni Memorial Hall or the Museum of Art

48. Whistler

49. The Fishbowl

50. University Hall

51. Mason Hall is named after Stevens T. Mason, the former governor of Michigan and the first president of the Board of Regents

Campus Tour Guide — Answers

52. False; it was the first.

53. e) all of the above

54. It was destroyed by fire on June 6, 1950.

55. a) Lorch Hall

56. Lorch Hall was designed by the first dean of architecture, Emil Lorch, as the first building for the sole purpose of instruction in architecture. The columns on the grounds are examples of the classical influence on American architecture.

57. The first modular research lab was temporarily built in the Lorch Hall garden.

58. The Harlan Hatcher Graduate Library

59. The Chicago World's Fair

60. Angell Hall

61. James B. Angell, president of the University from 1871 to 1909

62. "Artes, Scientia, Veritas," the school motto

63. "Religion, morality, and knowledge,

167

being necessary to good government and the happiness of mankind, schools and the means of education shall forever be encouraged," from the Ordinance of 1787 which established the Northwest Territory

64. Angell Hall

65. The Modern Language Building

66. William L. Clements Library

67. Professor Ulrich B. Phillips, a historian on the University faculty in 1923

68. The Harlan Hatcher Graduate Library

69. In front of the William L. Clements Library

70. Junius Emery Beal was an Ann Arbor businessman, publisher and politician, and a regent of the University of Michigan.

71. **Two Open Triangles Up Gyratory II** (1982)

72. Behind the Gerald R. Ford Library on North Campus

73. 150 pounds
74. George Rickey
75. "Arb"
76. The Dental Building
77. "The Tooth Fairy"
78. molar
79. **Gemini IV**, June 3-7, 1965
80. Doctor of Astronautical Science
81. The Power Center for the Performing Arts
82. three million
83. Picasso
84. William W. Cook
85. self-contained
86. Cook died of tuberculosis before the Law Quad was completed.
87. The architecture of the Law Quad resembles the Tudor-Gothic style of Oxford, Cambridge, and the Inns
88. "Diag"

Campus Tour Guide — Answers

of Court in London. The Lawyers Club Tower is similar to the entrance of the Clock Court in Hampton Court Palace, and the dining hall resembles the Kings College Chapel in Cambridge.

89. Martha Cook Residence

90. As a social answer to the all-male law school

91. The death of a female student from Asia caused him to take immediate action to improve the poor living situations of female students.

92. His mother

93. Supposedly, if a student steps on the bronze seal he or she will fail the first exam.

94. Behind the Harlan Hatcher Graduate Library in the center of the Diag

95. The Class of 1953

96. 72,000

97. Michigan beat Ohio Wesleyan, 33-0.

98. d) 97,239

99. False, 1956

Campus Tour Guide — Answers

100. Crisler Arena

101. H.O. Fritz Crisler, football coach and athletic director

102. Peace Corps

103. The Union (The quote is from a plaque on the building.)

104. Ann B. Davis, of "The Brady Bunch"

105. **Time**

106. Ritter Span

107. President James Burill Angell

108. In 1880 President Hayes appointed Angell minister to China to negotiate an immigration treaty. In 1887 President Cleveland appointed him to serve on the Northwestern Fisheries Commission and as a member of the Canadian-American Deep Waterways Commission. In 1897 he was asked by President McKinley to serve as special envoy and minister plenipotentiary to Turkey.

109. Angell wanted to retire at seventy-

Campus Tour Guide — Answers

six but the Regents declined his wish until four years later.

110. Washington's Birthday

111. Michigan versus Minnesota at Detroit, 1897

112. Louis Elbel 1899 wrote it after an 1898 triumph over Chicago. "The Victors" was rated as the "best college march ever written" by John Philip Sousa.

113. Madelon Stockwell

114. She was the first female student, entering the University as a sophomore, February 1870.

115. Wide receiver

116. Most all-purpose yardage per player and second highest number of touchdown passes caught

117. Michigan Panthers

118. The Ann Arbor Summer Festival

119. Glenn E. "Bo" Schembechler

120. 100th

121. He was chosen National Coach of the Year.

Campus Tour Guide — Answers

122. Lantern Night

123. The University women

124. Seniors passed lighted lamps to juniors who, in turn, passed garlanded hoops to sophomores. The freshman women then presented a play to all the members.

125. President Gerald R. Ford '35, 38th president of the United States (1974-1977)

126. Center

127. Delta Kappa Epsilon

128. "The Victors"

129. The Alumni Center

130. The first University of Michigan class to graduate, August 6, 1845

131. The **Michigan Alumnus**

MICH MOSH

1. What was billed as the "most significant event in the history of Michigan coeducation"?

2. Which campus building was built in 1891 and was originally the home of Regent Charles Adolphus Whitman?

3. Alice Crocker Lloyd Hall was named after the _____ of women.

4. Why was a dorm named after Mary Elizabeth Butler Markley?

5. The School of Education is located in the former University elementary

and secondary _____ schools.

6. _____, designed in 1904 by George Mason and Albert Kahn, is the oldest engineering building on campus and the oldest in the history of engineering education in the United States.

7. In what year was the East Engineering Building built?

8. A 1913 request of President Harry Burns Hutchins for relief of crowded classroom space resulted in the state legislature's gift of the Edward Henry Kraus _____ Building.

9. Who was Edward Henry Kraus?

10. The Undergraduate Library, better known as the UGLI, was the ____ library in the United States to be built for the sole use of undergraduates.

11. What do Grace Kelly, Jimmy Stewart and Helen Hayes have in common with the Michigan League?

12. The College of Pharmacy, founded in 1876, was the _____

college in the nation to offer a full-time university program in pharmacy.

13. The College of Pharmacy was originally the Chem-Pharmacy Building, built in 1856. It contained the first _____ at a state university, and in 1865 awarded the first pharmaceutical chemistry degrees.

14. What did the Samuel Trask Dana Natural Resources Building offer to students in the United States?

15. Mosher-Jordan Hall was named after Eliza M. Mosher and Myra B. Jordan, the first two deans of ____.

16. Where was the first University Hospital located in 1868?

17. The _____ House is used for official University functions.

18. For whom is the North Campus Bursley Dormitory named?

19. The University of Michigan biological station at Douglas Lake is the world's _____ inland field station for instruction and research in biological science.

20. For whom was the Baits Housing on North Campus named?

21. The Chase Osborn Preserve in Chippewa County of the Upper Peninsula was named after the regent of the University from 1908 to 1911 and Michigan's _____ governor.
    a) second
    b) eleventh
    c) sixtieth
    d) thirty-ninth

22. In the fall of 1985, how many students were enrolled at the University of Michigan?

23. Who stood in front of the Horace H. Rackham School of Graduate Studies on May 16, 1952, and praised the University for serving the world as a "symposium of art, culture, commerce and industry"?

24. In October 1911 what happened to the vault in the administrative offices of University Hall?

25. What is the oldest student organization, founded September 30, 1843, for the "purpose of general mental improvement"?

26. What do the letters of MUSKET,

the campus musical organization, represent?

27. Which campus organization includes a secret yearly Indian ritual?

28. This former United States President re-entered public life at the University of Michigan with a speech entitled "Sentiment in Our National Life" on February 22, 1892. President James Angell greeted this person at the train with a carriage and horses decorated in maize and blue. In his speech, he stated, "When I was in office and in need of help, I usually turned to the University of Michigan." Who is he?

29. When was the first issue of the **University of Michigan Daily** published?

30. What was the first newspaper to be edited in the Student Publications Building?

31. What did the commencement of the Class of 1937 celebrate?

32. What is the name of the University of Michigan yearbook?

33. Journalism professor Donald Ham-

ilton wrote _____, a novel set on the University campus.

34. In Angell Hall there is a bronze plaque on the floor commemorating the spot where the _____ of the Class of 1869 stood for over fifty years.

35. The _____, named after Dr. Carl E. Badgley, was developed to mend hip fractures.

36. The first _____ took place at the University of Michigan Hospital in 1968.

37. Why did the **Ann Arbor Times News** report that hundreds of University students left the campus with the coming of the 1910 Halley's Comet?

38. For what accomplishment did University faculty member F. Percival Price win the Pulitzer Prize in 1934?

39. Besides Ann Arbor, where are the two other University campuses located?

40. For whom is the cannon, donated by the Class of 1899, next to the Clements Library named?

179

Mich Mosh — Questions

41. To whom did President James B. Angell read a memorial on the banks of the Narragansett River in August 1885?

42. Which student hangout, located at 709 North University, exhibits 1920s-style decor and offers a varied selection of teas and candy?

43. Which French soprano made her first American Festival Concert debut at the 38th Annual May Festival of the University Musical Society at Hill Auditorium on May 13-16, 1931?

44. During the 1923 fall semester, the faculty and students of the College of Engineering built a 200-watt station in the West Engineering Building. With whom did the University establish a regular broadcasting series in 1925?

45. Name the source of the following statement: "The way I look at it, anybody who wants to be president should come to the University of Michigan and ask for your votes."

46. In the 1985 **Michigan Daily** special issue entitled "The Best of Ann Arbor," name the "Bests" in the following categories:

Mich Mosh — Questions

a) Ice cream
b) Deli
c) Breakfast spot
d) Place to take a first date
e) Place to take the folks
f) Late night eats
g) Bar atmosphere
h) Dance bar
i) Happy Hour
j) Thursday night spot
k) Place to be on a Saturday afternoon
l) Basketball game
m) Most awaited celebration
n) Day of classes
o) **Worst** line to wait on

47. What is the nickname of Ann Arbor?

48. What is the "Arcade" and where is it located?

49. Where is "Engine Arch" located?

50. True or False: LSA, or Literature, Science and the Arts, is the second largest college at the University.

51. In 1845 what crop covered the University?

52. Why was a wooden fence placed around the campus during the 1800s?

53. How many schools and colleges are located on the Ann Arbor campus?

54. Name the schools and colleges on the Ann Arbor campus.

55. Who designed the 1940 Thomas

181

M. Cooley Fountain, donated by Charles Baird and located between the Michigan League and the Burton Memorial Tower?

56. Which Greek god does this statue depict?

57. What was the original name of the statue?

58. What special quality does Hill Auditorium have?

59. What "project" on North Campus has existed for the last thirty years to find peaceful uses for atomic energy?

60. The University Medical Center contains the largest school of nursing and the first University _____ in the United States.

61. For whom is the University's Bentley Historical Library named?

62. For whom were the University's Jerome Lecture series on Roman and Greek studies named?

63. Who was the father of this alumnus?

64. Which two famous English authors wrote about this graduate's life

work on a Roman history book while he lived on the island of Capri?

65. What is the Barbour Scholarship, and who were its first recipients?

66. Which two former United States presidents chaired the November 1984 symposium on "New Weapons, Technologies and Soviet-American Relations" at the Rackham Graduate School?

67. The University of Michigan's C.S. Mott Children's Hospital was one of the recipients of money raised by the 1985 _____, which featured such celebrities as Bob Hope, Kenny Rogers, Diana Ross, Donny and Marie Osmond and Sparky Anderson.

68. What medical reporter often turns to the University Medical Center for stories which include "childhood obesity, cochlear implants to improve hearing and an interview with University of Michigan's ninth heart transplant patient"?

69. Who was the University Medical Center's first test-tube baby?

70. Which of the following terms

Mich Mosh — Questions

accurately describes the architecture of the University of Michigan?

a) Classical Revival
b) Romanesque
c) Gothic
d) Eclectic
e) Georgian
f) Modern
g) Renaissance

71. What is located on top of Peach Mountain in Stinchfield Woods, the School of Natural Resources' research forest?

72. On what three bodies of water in Ann Arbor may a University student canoe?

73. Where do University students often buy fruit, vegetables, flowers, handicrafts and baked goods?

74. At which major transportation center are University students seen in August, December and May?

75. Which Ann Arbor locale, at 1421 Hill Street, is the site of the Ann Arbor Folk Festival each January?

76. University students frequent a group of shops located in renovated buildings at 407 N. Fifth Avenue. What is the name of this complex?

77. Which University building, dedicated October 4, 1985, contains the

Julian and Vera McIntosh Theatre, The Blanche Anderson Moore Hall, the organ recital hall; and the Stearns Collection of Musical Instruments?

78. Which Ann Arbor shop, located on N. Fifth Avenue, is a favorite haunt of University students and alumni, especially the author's parents, for memorabilia and antiques?

79. Which two University School of Music professors recorded several albums together and drew 2,500 people to their July 4, 1985, Tanglewood concert?

80. Charles Owen served as a professor of music at the University of Michigan, the principal percussionist with the Philadelphia Orchestra from 1954 to 1972, and as the timpanist and marimba soloist from 1934 to 1954 for the _____.

81. This early professor, formerly the only mechanical engineer in Michigan, was sent by the navy to the University to teach steam engineering and iron shipbuilding in 1879. He chaired the Engineering Department in 1904 and was the first Dean of the College of Engineering in 1915. Who is he?

82. Which imprisoned South African anti-apartheid leader received an honorary degree in the Diag before the May 3, 1986, commencement by the Free South Africa Coordinating Committee?

ANSWERS

1. In response to the male-oriented Michigan Union, the Michigan League was specifically designed as a center for the cultural and social activities of women students, June 14, 1929.

2. The Institute of Human Adjustment, Counseling Division

3. dean

4. Markley was one of the first women to graduate from the University (1892).

5. laboratory

Mich Mosh — Answers

6. West Engineering Building

7. 1923

8. Natural Science

9. Edward Henry Kraus was the former dean of the College of Pharmacy, the Dean of the College of Literature, Science and Arts, and a distinguished mineralogist.

10. second

11. They each performed at the Lydia Mendelssohn Theatre and stayed overnight at the League.

12. first

13. chemistry laboratory

14. Regular instruction in forestry and conservation (at Stinchfield Woods, Camp Filibert Roth at Golden Lake Michigan and Douglas Lake)

15. women

16. The easternmost house facing North University Avenue served as the Dental Building in 1891 and was removed in 1908.

17. Inglis

Mich Mosh — Answers

18. Gilbert E. Bursley, a Republican state legislator from Ann Arbor; a member of the Michigan House of Representatives, 1960-1964; and a member of the Michigan Senate, 1964-1978

19. largest

20. Regent Vera B. Baits

21. d) thirty-ninth

22. 34,340 students

23. General Douglas MacArthur

24. The safe was blown open with nitroglycerin and three hundred dollars taken.

25. Alpha Nu

26. Michigan Union Show Ko-Eds Too

27. Michigama

28. President Grover Cleveland

29. September 1890

30. **Summer Michigan Daily**, (1932)

31. One hundred years of the University of Michigan on the Ann Arbor campus

Mich Mosh — Answers

32. The **Michiganensian**

33. **Shadow on the Campus**

34. elm tree

35. Badgley Pin

36. heart transplant

37. A University of Michigan astronomer announced that the tail of the comet contained cyanogen gas, which is a form of cyanide.

38. F. Percival Price, faculty member from 1939 to 1972 and international expert on capanology, or bell music, won the 1934 Pulitzer Prize for his "St. Lawrence Symphony." Price was the first professor of campanology in the United States, allowing the University the distinction of being the sole school to offer a degree in carillon performance.

39. Flint and Dearborn

40. The University of Michigan students who fought in the war with Spain

41. Ulysses S. Grant

42. Drake's Sandwich Shop

43. Lily Pons

44. WJR of Detroit

45. Walter Mondale, during an October 1984 presidential-race speech with Senator Gary Hart in the Diag

46. a) Steve's
    b) Zingerman's
    c) Angelo's
    d) Bicycle Jim's
    e) The Gandy Dancer
    f) PanTree
    g) Rick's
    h) The Nectarine Ballroom
    i) Rick's
    j) Charlie's
    k) The Arb
    l) Michigan 69, Iowa 67
    m) The first Detroit Tigers' World Series victory since 1968
    n) Last
    o) CRISP, Computer Registration Involving Student Participation

47. A^2

48. The Arcade is the pathway of shops leading from State Street to Maynard Street.

49. Engine Arch is located on the West Engineering Building at the southeast corner of the Diag.

Mich Mosh — Answers

50. False: LSA is the largest school.

51. Wheat

52. The fence enclosed the University cows and kept the local farmer's cows from entering.

53. Seventeen

54. School of Art
    College of Architecture and Urban Planning
    School of Business Administration
    School of Dentistry
    School of Education
    College of Engineering
    Rackham Graduate School
    Law School
    School of Library Science
    College of Literature, Science and the Arts
    Medical School
    School of Music
    School of Natural Resources
    School of Nursing
    College of Pharmacy
    School of Public Health
    School of Social Work

55. Carl Milles

56. Triton, god of the sea

57. **Sunday Morning**

58. Hill Auditorium is acoustically perfect.

59. Phoenix

60. Hospital

61. Alvin M. Bentley III, a former United States congressman, University regent and undergraduate history student

62. Thomas Spencer Jerome 1884

63. David H. Jerome, governor of the state of Michigan from 1881 to 1883

64. Comptom Mackenzie in **Vestal Fire** and Somerset Maugham in "Mayheu"

65. Levi Barbour, Law 1865 and former Regent, established this scholarship for women from all Eastern countries due to their lack of formal education in the late 1800s. Mutsu Kikuchi and Kameyo Sadakata were the first Barbour Scholars.

66. Gerald R. Ford and Jimmy Carter

67. "Children's Miracle Network Telethon"

68. Tom Marshall, WDIV-TV, Channel 4 Detroit

Mich Mosh — Answers

69. Jenafer Elisa Robichaud, daughter of Donna and Terry, born July 12, 1985, with the aid of the University of Michigan's Reproductive Endocrinology and Infertility Service

70. d) Eclectic

71. The WUOM, the University radio station, transmission tower

72. The Huron River, Argo Pond and Geddes Pond

73. Ann Arbor Farmer's Market

74. Detroit Metropolitan Airport

75. The Ark Coffeehouse

76. Kerrytown

77. Margaret Dow Towsley Center

78. The Treasure Mart

79. William Bolcom, Professor of Composition and Joan Morris, Adjunct Assistant Professor of Voice

80. United States Marine Band

81. Mortimer Cooley

82. Nelson Mandela